WINDOWS WIT

Insights of a Psychic Medium

By

Robert E. Hansen

Printed in the United States of America

First Printing, 2016

ISBN: 0692689516
ISBN-13 978-0692689516

1757 Merrick Ave
Suite 106
Merrick, NY 11566
516-868-7778

www.robertehansen.com

This book is dedicated to all those who have been abandoned by the world. The homeless, the destitute, the dying, the alcoholics, the addicts, the POWs, the MIAs, the mentally challenged, the lonely...

"Never deprive someone of hope... it might be all they have left."

- H. Jackson Brown. Jr.

Table of Contents

Foreword

When Robert first read me, my mother's voice came through him. I was shocked he could know so much. She's been my angel since she passed away three decades ago, but even going beyond that many people that claim to have the incredible gift Robert has use it solely to take advantage of the broken and the trusting. He helped me to find peace with my life-long bereavement.

Choosing to sit with Robert proved so rewarding to me. That's why I urged him to share this book. I don't feel he really understands how wonderful his words and gifts are.

This book will make you cry and smile. It provides the kind of simple sayings we need to hear and believe to come to terms with loss, whether by death or bad break up. Personally, Robert has helped me learn what it means to truly love and be loved.

Grief can be so devastating. Sadly, he understands loss himself all too well. His brother, father and young nephew were all taken too soon. When you read his positive affirmations, they will help settle your mind for and during those challenging times.

Whether you believe in mediums or not, you will find joy and wisdom here. You can read this book with hope or doubt and come out so much stronger. His beautiful words have always inspired and comforted me when things looked dismal.

Life is a beautiful, precious gift and I hope whatever your trial or tribulation, this book eases the pain and brings you comfort. We all have setbacks. We all grieve. But it's only part of the journey.

Hope you all enjoy this book and find comfort as well! As Robert would say...

Peace Always

Judy San Roman
Author, Filmmaker

Preface

The human experience is extraordinary and unique to each one of us. We interpret our experiences through our conditioning, our culture, genetics, fears, desires, religious or spiritual training and through our very souls. These moments move through our viscera as glints of light in the dark, both the sound of thunder and the quietest whispers.

They cannot be captured in words, thoughts or memories. Those are only replicas, mental cut outs of what was. All of our experiences, insights, joys, sufferings, successes or failures each unfold and then disappear, each moment dying and being reborn... Some try to hold on, others try to let go. For all... they remain the silent teachers pointing us home.

These are some of the things I have learned.

Over the past 25 years, I have spent much of my time working with people enduring the loss of loved ones, of pets and the challenges of special education children. I've been with others who are dealing with incurable illnesses, those who attend to the dying and others who are dying themselves. I have met so many who have great anxiety and fears, so many unable to shed grief or deal with their day to day suffering.

Their doubts and their fears overwhelm them.

Many are seeking hope. Others are seeking peace.

After a great many conversations with my family, friends, clients and many other wonderful people I have never met, I finally sat down and organized these passages that express my own personal journey. It is a journey that has crossed over many mountains and fallen into many valleys. These short essays and simple statements are reflections of my personal insights, each presented to me through the looking glass of my own soul.

I hope that you enjoy them, read them... then discard them.

For their only purpose is to point toward a direction of love and compassion, to come to see that what you seek is within... that you are love itself.

You are the peace that you have been searching for.

I would like to extend the deepest appreciation to my friend, business partner and companion on this amazing journey, Dominick Martini. It is his dedication, support and firm commitment that has brought this book to life...

From my heart I thank you.

For my wife Kathleen, thank you for your tireless effort, patience and direction in helping to prepare this book. Your insight and attention to detail has been invaluable. The essence of this work has been expressed with the written word through your inspiration...

All my love,

Robert E. Hansen

*

You are stronger than you think.
Look how much you have endured...

It is an honor to meet you.

*

The
Spiritual

Born in Spirit

Meditation and Intuition

The Deep Mind

The Deep Heart

Born in Spirit

We were born in the image of creation, endowed with the gifts of the universe. We have been placed in this extraordinary place we call home... with all its majesty.

We are the children and the parents.

We are birth and death.

We are the alpha and the omega. As it was in the beginning, so it is now, so it has always been.

No payment required, no debt owed.

It is all free to us. It has always been in front of us. We do not have to search for it. It is right here.

So simple!

Why do we not see it? Why do so many seek and not find?

*

The sun is warm, the air full of summer. The sound of birds wake the day, waves returning to shore and salt water bubbles play in the sand.

The landscape colored by the brushstroke of the One Artist, each moment the only moment.

Yours...

No matter what your world has brought you it has also given you this.

I bend my knee in thanks.

*

When your mind opens, you see the One everywhere.

When your heart opens, you feel the One within.

When your soul opens, you become of the One.

Have you found the path to what opens these doors?

We often take things for granted. It is a form of vanity, an expectation...

It is slow working venom that over time spawns greed, envy and jealousy.

Taking things for granted drives pain into those we come in contact with, those whom we love...

This is why we must reclaim ourselves.

We must stop and really look. We must witness ourselves unfold perfectly, the gift of life with all its joy and all its pain revealing itself...

Do not pray for an easy life.

Pray for the strength to live each of those moments as they unfold no matter that joy or sorrow and pain.

A miracle lives through each one of us. The very presence of the One Life flows through us all... Nothing is more important to the Beloved than you.

So at your time of rest, take a moment. Place your hands over the center of your heart. Be still, silent and breathe easy while whispering the words...

"I am grateful."

Your soul will be very proud of you.

*

Never confuse the label with the truth, the idea with the direct experience, the word for the unspoken silence, and understanding for inner wisdom...

The idea of love for Love... the thought of God as God...

It must become a radiant truth that is unshakable, vibrant and real.

*

If only once...

You have brought comfort to one person.

You have offered your hands and heart without pause.

You have reached down to lift another, to help another to climb higher than you can reach.

You have brought compassion to the dying, to those who suffer, to the scared and broken.

You have placed yourself next to the dying to hold their hand as the Angel of Death arrives.

If you have done any of these, even only once... you have chosen a path of Grace.

You have chosen a journey of the heart that every soul in Heaven will sing in praise.

*

Diving

I dove deep into the water of my soul, a pure liquid sprinkled by the remaining sunlight. A dying heat casts its fingers upon the surface, pleading with the waves to ebb and flow calmly without chop or sound. The clouds above disappeared from view, patches of thought like white clouds trying to remain in sight, the stars trying to guide my compass being overtaken by thunderheads rising miles into the horizon.

The storm was close. The boom and flash of thunder and lightning drove me deeper. My lungs filled with air, holding to all I have unlearned, emptying memory and emptying myself.

My sense of self unraveled in the squall of this personal ocean. My compass broken, I strained for the seagull, a sight of land. A bell rang, not from the ocean buoy, but the tones from within my own mind straining to guide me to a shore that cannot be seen or heard across the twisted debris of broken dreams. The corpses of my many lives waved in recognition.

My lungs stretched to burst, my soul kicked hard. No surface in sight, I was about to surrender to it all...

And then from nowhere a hand reached deep into the water and brought me to the surface...

His hair long, eyes light blue, I have seen him before. I know his voice. The hands of a fisherman pull me into a boat with twelve others, nets cast about, fear cast aside.

"I am with you," he said.

*

You have been given the gift of life... that is how deeply you are loved in Spirit.

You are its child.

Be the echo of the Spirit's great love.

*

It is the resistance to the suffering of grief that binds you in sorrow. It is the fear that you will be forced to rise again, that your naked feet would bear the thorns of the world and your tired eyes would turn away from the mirror of your soul...

When you accept fully that you are heartbroken a Gift of Grace will enter. The demons will find no quarter within your heart...

They will run screaming from your soul, cast back into darkness in which they were born.

Divine light will have found its way home and grace will heal your wounds...

You will come to find the rest you seek as love songs whisper into your heart.

*

Pray to them with all your heart.

Tell them that you miss them.

They can hear your heart calling.

It is through the open window of your soul that they return to you.

13

*

Two Angels

At the heart of grief you will find a sharp and painful focus on what is absent, what is missing... what is lost.

The Angel of Grief always carries with it the destruction of what you "hoped would be" or what "should have been." It casts a powerful light that brings to ashes all that you thought you could control, contain and hold on to. It is the great teacher that empties us of our fantasy and illusions. It serves to humble us, to bring us to the knees of our souls...

The Angel of Grief always travels with its twin... The Angel of Healing.

The Angel of Healing teaches us to shift from what was... to what is.

From the darkness of absence to the awe of presence.

From what has been lost to what has never been lost.

From death to life.

From lost love to continued love in the face of loss.

From thoughts of Hell to the presence of Heaven.

These Angels invite us to be where our loved ones are, to be here now and return to the center of your heart...

*

Fear always arises in the darkness of confusion, the thoughts of bad endings and painful conclusions...

There is no ending. Fear not.

Born out of grace and compassion, your divine soul knows not of fear. It is always being called to its eternal home... to your Spirit's Great Love.

Say your prayers.

*

Look closely into the eyes of a child.

The brilliance of Love will fill your own vision...

The light that you see is the Spirit reminding you of how loved you are.

Listen with your heart.

You will hear the voice of Love calling you...

It is the voice of the Beloved reminding you of how precious you are...

How sacred you are.

*

Those whom we love that die unexpectedly plead for us to live each moment fully, the light and wisdom of their souls pointing to this and every moment.

*

Prayer and meditation are not techniques to be practiced.

They are expressions of great love. They are silent voices spoken from your soul. They do not create dependence, neediness or ritual.

Rather, they serve as love letters straight to the Heart of the Beloved...

To the presence of your Spirit.

*

Every moment is a living prayer... a devoted brushstroke to the masterwork of the One Artist.

Do your best... that is all that is asked of us.

*

When you are fully ready you will feel a release.

A freedom will awaken within you.

It will remove your denial of the unchangeable past. It will come as a Gift of Grace, a complete acceptance of their journey and yours.

*

Renew yourself in the miracle of self-love, self-forgiveness and self-compassion...

It is given to you freely by the Beloved.

You are the answer to your prayers... that is how much love and trust the Beloved has in you.

*

We have been given to each other to offer our strength, our compassion and love...

Without these we are lost.

Meditation and Intuition

In spiritual circles it is often suggested that one must come to accept the moment.

The thought of acceptance is non-acceptance...

The thought of Love is not Love.

*

The secret to dealing with pain...

Do you remember when you would play in the snow? When you would play freely for hours until the sun went down, and your mother would finally call you into the house?

You would go into the bathroom or the kitchen sink and run your frozen hands under the hot water...

Boy, it hurt like hell and stung big time.

Now imagine if someone from another land was watching this painful scene. Eventually they would stop you and ask...

"Doesn't that hurt your hands...?"

"Yes," you would answer. "It does. But while my hands may hurt for a bit I know they are returning to normal. This pain is part of my healing. I am returning back to myself."

Do not be so quick to get away from your pain or discomfort... As some say, the road to Heaven goes through Hell. Pain is necessary for recovery. When you allow it to be... the hidden gift of Grace will show itself.

The light of peace and healing will then shine through.

*

Meditation is neither the practice of getting somewhere special, nor disappearing from the world.

It is not a clever way to re-invent ourselves as spiritual, unique or different.

It is a simple surrender.

It is to return home to our natural state of being.

It is to realize, deeply, the incredible truth of what we are... creation itself in all its wonder.

*

I try to take a walk every day. I began this as a daily practice some years ago, a meditation if you will.

In my early years I realized I was either always walking towards or away from something...

But never just walking!

I would be in the most beautiful areas, all the brilliance of the planet Earth showing herself off in vibrant tones, colors and sounds.

As I walked I would be paying my bills in my head, having debates with my family or answering my cell phone.

I would be caught in the non-stop mind stream of thought, a constant movement of distraction.

The one thing I was not doing was walking!

My legs were moving. My body was pressed into exercise... I would become tired and sweaty.

But I was not walking. I was in a trance, looking to hurry and be done so I could move onto the next thing to *do*.

"How was your walk?" My kids would ask me.

Lying to myself I would say, "Oh, it was great!"

A great spiritual teacher was once asked...

"What powers do you have?"

"When I eat," she answered, "I just eat. When I drink, I just drink. And when I walk... I just walk. I do not wobble!"

As I was walking today, in the great silence of the morning, I saw beautiful geese creating a circle around their babies. They waved their huge wings, protecting and celebrating them.

The trees just gave birth to their children, each new leaf, each radiant petal, lifting itself in thanks.

The blackbirds, the blue jays, the robin redbreasts, all living their lives in a performance of song like many diamonds sparkling in the sun.

I finally went for a walk today.

*

Take time with yourself to be alone.

Learn to be at peace within...it is only when you can truly stand within your own soul that you can truly fall in love...

Otherwise you will never know if you fell in love because you are lonely and afraid of being by yourself.

*

Our group sat in meditation.

For some this is a chore to be done, a task to be ticked off or burden carried...

For others it is a welcoming surrender, a release of effort and relinquishing of control...

Each receives what they ask for.

*

Doubt

There are many people who step into the day full of doubt and hesitation...

They see themselves questioning everything.

"I'm not sure what the weather will do. I always feel they are lying. I know the people at work may not like me. The neighbors are always looking through their windows, judging me. Do I look good enough to go out for dinner? I'm sure he was just pretending to like me..."

So it goes and goes.

"Do you love yourself?" Doubt itself was asked once.

Doubt thought about it.

"I'm not sure..."

There is the source of all suffering.

*

The Zen master asked: "Do you have a past?"

"Yes, I have a past," the student exclaimed.

"Is that so," said the Zen master. "Then bring me your past if you have one. I want to see it!"

The Zen master asked: "Do you have a future?"

"Yes, I have a future," the student shouted.

"Wonderful," said the teacher. "Show it to me, if you have your future. I want to touch it!"

With great compassion the Zen master looked into the eyes of his student.

"Young woman, do you not see that you only have this divine moment? And no matter what story of the past you tell yourself or what imagination creates your future, it is but a story, a dream?"

At that moment the student heard the sound of a blackbird singing.

Nothing more needed be said.

*

The Buddha taught that suffering is caused by two great sorrows.

One is fear, the other wanting.

Fear of change, fear of the unexpected, of loss, death, rejection, fear of having fear and on...

Seeking, demanding, wanting something you cannot have... Wanting something that you have and are afraid of losing... Wanting to be free of something that you did not ask for and being forced to accept it...

This is the source of all suffering.

There is a way out...

Have you found it?

*

A Meditation Tip

Often during meditation negative or disturbing thoughts can arise... At times even fearful thoughts may enter. For many practitioners they will flee from these negative emotions.

They will disconnect the meditation and walk away.

Simply allow the thoughts to be. Stay with the fear and sit with this "disease." Do not react.

This is called Maya, the great trickster, tempter and illusionist that makes it seem real.

Look Maya in the "eye," unflinching, settled and present.

You will find that your transcendental presence will shine through. A light will penetrate this darkness. This mind construct will start to dissolve and the peace that passes all understanding will reveal itself...

The Light of the Spirit will shine through... and Maya will dissolve into emptiness.

Remember... Your fear is only as large as your avoidance of it.

*

Nirvana.

So often the term has been misused or misunderstood.

Literally translated, it means "cessation" or "the end of..."

In spiritual practice Nirvana refers to the end of suffering, the end of the wheel of the continuous cycle of fear and wanting... It is not a place to go, not a location. It is the brilliant clarity of your "true nature."

It is the end of confusion... Nirvana is freedom.

*

Namaste is a spiritual term often spoken by both westerners and easterners these days. When spoken, hands are often brought to the heart level (heart chakra) and compressed briefly into a prayer position.

A slight bow is taken... followed by the spoken word "Namaste."

Often thought a "new age" greeting, Namaste is in truth quite old. Beautiful and very respectful, it simply and deeply means...

"I honor the God light that lives within you."

In this very simple tribute one person facing the other honors the One Life in both of them, the One Life in us all...

Namaste is the highest form of respect and prayer.

When sincerely spoken it is a living meditation... an arrival of God consciousness, truly presence honoring itself.

*

Invitation to the Suffering

Consider the possibility that within your suffering... you are being given an invitation to let go of all of your expectations, desires and wants.

You are being allowed to release the demands of "what should have been."

You are being welcomed to rise from the dream, to embrace life in all its broken wonder... to fall in love with where you are, to be fully present and to come to see that your beautiful heart is being healed no matter how wounded you may feel...

*

The purpose of meditation, contemplation and prayer is not to escape the challenges of life by creating an alternative world built upon psychic and spiritual fantasy. It is not to wait to be saved or rescued, to use mystical and magical thinking to avoid the present expression of your life as it is...

Rather...

Its true purpose is to penetrate the illusion of those fantasies, to reveal the essence of what and who you truly are, to free you from self-bound thought and to come to a deep peace in realizing on the most intimate level that you are a child of the divine.

To know your place in the human experience is not only extraordinary... but that you are a creation by the God Essence...

That is how precious and important you are... right here and now!

*

Before you enter the day, take a few moments... even if it's just one.

Relax your breath. Give yourself a chance to really breathe easy, slowly...

This allows the mind to settle down...

Be still. Carry on.

*

Perfection in Spiritual Imperfection

There is a great misunderstanding that moves among many spiritual practitioners and citizens on the "path."

They see their foolishness, clumsiness and imperfections as failures, as non-spiritual. They feel their anxieties and doubts have no part in the spiritual journey...

Friends, there is a great freedom in embracing your humanity, your *humanness*, with all of its beautiful flaws and imperfections.

23

Accepting yourself in these moments as you are, completely and fully, *is the spiritual path.*

Bow to your flaws. Honor the wrinkles that form on your spiritual skin. Feel free with your blemishes...

Don't blind yourself with spiritual hypnosis or fantasy.

Be fully aware of your "imperfections." Take a drink from the worn clay pot with all its flaws and cracks, its stains and fading color... How beautiful!

When you accept yourself fully in the presence of this moment with all of your shattered edges and shaking hands... it makes you honest. Genuine. Sincere... Real!

It's nice to meet you.

This is the Spiritual way.

*

Are you willing to look at yourself deeply?

Without self judgement? Without minimizing or inflating yourself? Without hiding or being defensive? Without fantasy? Aggression or fear?

Are you willing to look... simply to see what is there?

*

A great Indian warrior walked the forest with his young son.

They came upon a fox slowly moving in the bramble. Its fur was thick, for snow was falling.

The fox's bright eyes pierced the shadows and he shot like an arrow in pursuit of his prey, a snowshoe rabbit.

Sensing the danger the snowshoe bolted into a run, its powerful legs driving the ice and snow out from under its feet.

"Now that the race has begun," the warrior asked his son, "who will win?"

"Father," he answered, "we all know that the sly fox will outrun the snowshoe rabbit."

The wise father smiled. He looked the son in the eyes.

"The snowshoe will win this race... today."

"Why father?" The son asked, confused.

"Remember, son. The fox is running for his dinner. The rabbit is running for his life."

*

A young man seeking the path of enlightenment was assigned his new teacher.

Upon meeting him, the young student realized his new teacher was completely blind. Unsure of what a blind man could "show him" the new student asked: "Of all things, master, to be blind must be the worst!" The master smiled and laughed.

"I see with my ears and listen with my eyes."

Thinking the master was mocking him, the young student became upset. The master immediately sensed this. He offered a brief demonstration.

"Young man, can you hear the cricket resting by your foot?"

The young student thought this to be silly, but to humor his teacher he looked down. To his astonishment there rested a cricket.

"Master! How is that you can hear this cricket?"

He smiled.

"Young man... how is it that you cannot?"

*

Choosing a Path

Do not worry about those who walk the path of truth, compassion and love...

Worry about those who walk the path of hate, deception and indifference.

Pay attention... Not all who you meet seek peace.

Holding On

Fear does not contain you... you contain fear.

Anger does not hold you... you hold anger.

Thoughts do not define you... they rise and fall.

Feelings do not hold you... they flow in and out like waves breaking on a distant shore...

Remember... you are Love itself. And only Love can hold you still.

*

"I have journeyed far," began the young apprentice. "My feet are blistered, my bones are brittle and I can no longer continue."

As he rested at the shoreline of a great river, he looked for a way of getting to the other side. The river was wide and deep. There was no way in sight.

He noticed a Zen monk sitting on the other shore.

"How can I get to the other side? He yelled across the water.

The Zen monk then saw the young traveler from across river and yelled back.

"You are on the other side."

The traveler immediately awakened.

*

Seeking Another

So many people I meet are seeking relationships...

They openly seek another person, looking, acting and role playing what they believe will be attractive to the "other."

They hope they will "find" that moment, that magical person, to complete and fulfill them.

Remember. When there is a great longing, a thirst of the heart and a hunger of the soul...

Be careful.

"A starving dog," my Zen master would so bluntly often say, "will eat poisoned food."

You may be satisfied temporarily... but, in a short time, sickness and death of the body and soul will follow.

When you are settled and clear, a true partner with yourself, then and only then can you be open to the joy of love and the love within another...

*

A great deal can be learned by watching flowers. When ready, they blossom.

Then they die.

No holding back, no resistance.

*

It was a quiet evening, right outside San Francisco. I sat in the Zendo, a place of meditation.

The center was hidden away, upon a beautiful lake. The air smelled of wood burning. The embers of the fire in the meditation hall jumped about, announcing themselves to the evening guests.

A conversation about death came up.

"What happens when we die?" Someone asked my Zen master.

"It will take some time to answer that question," he reflected.

He provided no direct answer.

Instead he placed a glass of clear water, filled to the top, next to his small night table.

A week went by. We had forgotten about the glass.

Before our meditation session began, he took a pencil from the table and tapped what was now an empty glass. The sound was sharp.

"The water in this glass is just like your human experience," he said. "In time it will be reabsorbed back into the One. Your death will come as the glass empties of water."

As the evening moved on it began to rain.

The Zen Master moved the glass through the open window and it filled with water. He laughed.

"See," he said, "you have returned."

*

The heart of the child reveals the path.

There is more than one way of looking at your world...

Celebrate... seek peace.

*

Excited to show her the wonder and beauty of nature, two parents took their very young child out for a walk one day in an open field.

A beautiful winged creature flew right past them. The parents quickly pointed it out.

"Look at the lovely bird!"

As it turns out a spiritual teacher had quietly been watching.

He closed his eyes and sighed quietly.

"By calling it a bird," he exclaimed to the parents, "your daughter will never see a bird again."

*

You will know you are on the right path... when that one in front of you begins to disappear.

*

Do not seek enlightenment because others have told you to do so...

Let it blossom... because you sense it growing within you.

*

Exhale. You have traveled far.

Place your burdens down for a while.

Rest easy.

The Deep Mind

Can you *feel* the moment when day shifts to night? When you move from wakefulness into sleep? From thought to silence? When you are truly still?

It is in these moments when your doorways open into emptiness. Pay attention to your senses, your past thoughts and examinations.

There are sights you have not seen that can be seen...

There are sounds you have not heard that can be heard...

Conceptions you have not conceived but can.

This is not metaphor.

This is not faith or belief... but direct experience.

Have you come upon it?

*

Man cannot create silence.

Man can become quiet.

Man creates *noise*.

Noise interrupts the Voice of the Spirit.

Can you find the doorway into silence?

To hear the Eternal One Voice?

*

All sound is born through its mother, Silence.

When sound subsides silence once again reveals herself, eternal, present and unending. The movement of the mind is quite like this. We do not notice the silence when we are fully engaged in thought.

As we allow mind noise to subside, to exhaust itself, the wisdom of the silent mother is felt...

Silence will speak. And she will smile... knowing the chatter of the mind is the playground from which she calls her children "home" and gives them love and rest.

*

As it is...

Looked for it cannot be seen... listened for it cannot be heard... felt for... it moves unnoticed.

And yet it is of all things. It is the flame within the fire, the light that darkness cannot consume... It is the life within the death, the death within the life.

An old friend calls me "home."

I close my eyes in gratitude.

Namaste.

*

If you live in darkness... even your shadow can not survive.

*

The Fine Lines

There is a fine line between enabling... and providing support.

There is a fine line between taking a break from overwhelming grief... and withdrawing and hiding.

There is a fine line between self-honesty and self-delusion.

There is a fine line between true love and the idea of true love.

There is a fine line between tough love and rejection.

There are so many fine lines...

As we meditate, pray and find the courage to ask hard questions about ourselves, we become more aware, still and quiet.

The fine lines will grow clearer, the choices more focused. Your decisions will be based on love and stillness, not upon control and fear.

You cannot have inner freedom while asking for inner safety.
They stand opposite to each other. The choice is yours.

*

Be still among the trees and stars. Listen carefully to their silent voices...
You stand among them a reminder of how sacred you are.

*

Remember that every experience, every emotion, every thought and every event no matter how small, no matter how large, no matter how wonderful or how tragic have all led you to this very moment...
To this one moment in your life.
To where you are.
Do you accept it fully or do you reject it fully?
Choose which path.
Acceptance or rejection.
No variations. It's gut check time.

*

It is easy to speak of what you might do... of what you might become.
It is easy to speak of what you have done... of what you have achieved.
Memories, words, thought... they all come and go.
They are the amusements of the mind that keep us walking around the edges of our lives.
Is it not time to fall completely into the center of your life?
Oh, to be here now!

*

When some people remember their past, they feel a sense of ease. For others, a sense of torment.

Both serve as our teachers. They point to freedom.

*

You need look no further than this moment... Everything here and now points to home.

Every thought, fear, embrace, tear and broken heart...

Every kiss and every prayer... It all points to this moment.

Everything has its roots in this present moment, calling you back to this spiritual truth.

When you let go of your separate self... you will come to see that your search ends where it has begun.

*

Your birth arrives in one moment.

Your passing arrives in one moment.

You find love in one moment.

You heart can break in one moment.

Freedom is found in one moment...

Stay present... you never know what this moment will bring.

*

True freedom is an internal awareness. It is a return to your natural state of consciousness. It is a shift, a movement from within that is not created by thoughts or ideas of places to go or some form of confidence or challenging of oneself in life threatening events.

It is not found by staying or leaving a particular location or person. It is not based on avoidance, nor does it disguise itself at the beach or in the woods.

It is not found hiding under the covers or disappearing into meditation or some other form of ritual. It is not found in a practice designed to take you out of the moment.

Freedom is not a practice of hiding, avoiding or deception no matter how clever, perfumed or passionate...

Those are forms of escape. And like any prisoner who escapes, you are always caught looking over your shoulder, never truly at peace.

Where then is freedom...?

*

Can you step into the coolness of this morning and truly know that this is the day? That this is the moment that life itself has created? That you are part of its wonder?

Can you feel your being in this moment, the only moment you can have?

Can you sense this? Despite whatever challenge lies in front of you? Can you feel this, even though heartache is with you? Even though disappointment has its hold on you?

Know this. You are life itself in all its wonder. No mystery, no secret...

You are life.

What you are struggling with is your resistance to life itself.

Let go for a while. Breathe deep.

This is your moment.

*

People say it is the light that casts my shadow...

People say it is my feet that create the dance...

It is the light of joy... the light of the Creator that casts the shadow...

And it this love song of light that moves my soul.

*

Your divine soul is always seeking reunion with the Beloved...

It hears the call to return home...

Love always finds a way.

*

Learn to be still. There is great strength in it.

*

Window

Take a few moments and be still...

Just let your thoughts come and go. Do not try to control them. Slowly bring your attention to your breathing...

Just pay attention to your breath. Two minutes... maybe three. That's all it takes.

Feel your grief. Feel the love. Let it flow like the wind through an open window.

Tears may fall... Let it be.

Anger may rise... Let it be.

Fear may enter... Let it be.

Joy may rise... Let it be.

This is the great healing. To accept, to allow, to deny nothing... within this act of complete surrender those who you love will enter through the window of your soul, their peace kissing your wounds...

It is their light guiding you to rest.

*

Butterflies do not know how beautiful their wings are... but human eyes do.

The waterfall does not realize the radiance of its voice... but human ears do.

It is the same with you.

You may never know the healing that your heart and soul brings to another... but they surely do.

Be at peace and carry on.

*

Being at peace is easy... it is staying there that you resist.

*

The moon filters in and out... The night air whistles cold...

Step out into it. Breathe deeply...

Give thanks... then rest.

*

Surrender and Resistance

Physical resistance builds muscle and increases endurance.

Spiritual resistance builds sorrow and increases separation.

In athletics, we never surrender... we may be defeated, but we never surrender.

In finding freedom on the spiritual path... surrender is the most important act.

That which you resist grows stronger within you.

The more you avoid what frightens you... the more its power grows and the more it controls your very being.

The greater the fear, the smaller your world... the smaller your self becomes.

The more you hold your breath... the more you'll find yourself at unease.

A great, often stated spiritual axiom says...

"You can run... but you cannot hide."

From what do you hide...?

Do you have the courage to come out of hiding...?

*

Fear arrives when thought overtakes presence... and soul.

*

In speaking of the elements of the world, the ancients would describe them as personalities.

The Earth was firm, settled and unmoving. Present and trustworthy, it was family.

The Water was flowing and adaptive. It ever sought and found the lowest forms. And yet it could wear away anything.

The Fire... Exciting, aggressive and passionate, it was quick to enter the fray, always hotheaded and courageous.

The Wind... Hard to hold, forever moving in all directions. Circling and shifting, it was the mysterious wanderer.

And the Void. Emptiness. Looked for but cannot be seen, evasive, secret and constantly shifting, it is egoless and silent.

*

Communication with those we love who have crossed over often occurs when we sleep.

Our loved ones penetrate the veil of thought when our conscious thinking has subsided, resistance has softened and the "inner window" opens...

I have met countless people who have had remarkable expressions of contact while dreaming.

*

That which you "seek" has never been lost...

Your mind has tricked you into believing that you have misplaced it.

Psychic energy is a part of each and every one of us. It has an energy field, a life of its own. It inhabits all creatures in both worlds... the manifested (the world of form) and the unmanifested (the world of no form, silence and space).

Both worlds exist; form in constant change, in flux and shifting, constantly embracing the cycle of birth and death. All things end and are reborn.

Emptiness (space) and stillness (no thought) are the two energy fields that remain as constant fluid movement. They exist with each other, connected not separate. It is within this empty stillness that thoughts move, light travels and sound is heard. It is where residence is taken after death (change) occurs. It is the one life standing before you always.

In emptiness, in stillness, energy such as wind, air, light, sound, thought, feelings, emotions, dreams and so on are all experienced in stillness, in silence, in emptiness. It is here where one must journey.

You cannot hold psychic energy, touch, box or grasp it. And yet it affects us, shifts us, and moves us in many directions. It is very powerful, very real and can be felt and known.

Its vast secrets are available. Try to discover a sense of it! It is not lost, only unrecognized.

Once you have had a true psychic experience, a genuine sense of it, it is unmistakable and undeniable (except by those who have not had it).

It can be tapped into.

This is not about believing. It is about coming to discover what is obvious yet so often missed.

*

Sit quietly and place the "ear" of your soul against the "conch shell..."

What or who would you listen for?

Guidance? The voice of a loved one? What the future holds?
And so on.

Listen carefully.

*

Living is easy... it's thinking that makes it hard.

*

It is not death that you fear.

It is the thought of death, the thought of ending that frightens you.

When death arrives it will come and leave before the movement of one breath...

It is within that space that the Eternal has arrived.

The Messenger has embraced its sacred child and the dear one has been welcomed home.

*

When you are truly thirsty, talk of water will not work. Thoughts of water are insufficient. Images of water will leave you parched... Only real water can cure your thirst.

It is the same with Love.

Love always penetrates sorrow as light always penetrates darkness.

*

If you are not present... you are absent.

*

The distance between the head and the heart is only 18 inches.

For some that journey takes a lifetime...

The Deep Heart

Be gentle on yourself.

Be compassionate to yourself.

If you could react differently, think differently, feel differently...

You would.

Remember...

All saints were once sinners.

*

There are those who are fearful and weak in their souls, who hold close to revenge, anger and jealousy. They wave dull blades, threatening anyone who stands near their trembling hearts.

Truly brave people embrace compassion and forgiveness. Their swords remain sheathed until they have no choice but to reveal their power.

*

The reasons why we suffer...

To love something and you cannot have it... we suffer.

To love something and be afraid of losing it... we suffer.

To want to be done with something but unable to free yourself from it... we suffer.

To endure an unwanted event and struggle from it... we suffer.

Why then do you suffer...?

Do you know the way out...?

To freedom... peace?

To joy?

*

The Trickster

Avoidance, denial, fantasy, resistance, blame, complaint and fear... these are the unique tools of the *egoic mind*.

The mental wizard, the "trickster," he laughs at how well his juggling act keeps us distracted... the court jester confusing the king.

These are thoughts that keep us away from "home," the movement of mind that blocks the light of your soul, your essence and your divine wonder... the presence of the One Life.

What to do? What to do...?

*

No matter the grief, the heartbreak and the loss, there are so many willing to offer comfort and compassion, the strength of their souls... for they too understand your pain and your sorrow. They too have been on a bed of nails. They too have watched the sky fall and the oceans turn into the abyss.

Speak of your grief. Speak of your anguish, not as an apology, not holding back in fear of opinion or judgement... Share it with those who truly love you, those who stand by you and those who do not watch the clock or offer boredom as a relief...

Speak until you cannot. Cry until the tears ask to stop... It is only then that healing can begin.

If there is no one to bring you comfort, know we are here, I am here and most importantly recall the ever presence of the loving Spirit.

Never forget you are loved more than you can ever know.

*

Everything that you know was at one time unknown to you.

This is the magic of being granted life... to fall into the unknown, carried by the breath of the One Life.

Worry not.

Karma...

If you were not supposed to be there... why were you?

If it was not supposed to happen to you... why did it?

If you could have acted any other way you would have!

Can you not see? Can you not recognize that the unfolding of your life, the very essence of your experiences, is intended to free you? To awaken you?

It is in this realization that self-forgiveness and self-compassion are offered... All that has occurred is unchanging, unshifting and it is in this light and acceptance that the darkness of worry, loss and heartbreak will be brought to ease...

Then the great gift of peace will enter.

*

The way through the grief... *is* the grief.

Cry often. Get angry. Enjoy small moments of peace when they arise. Set aside pride. Ask for help. Be gentle on yourself. Cry again. Yell out loud. Deny nothing of what you feel. Pray often. Take care of your health. Rest when you can.

Try not to reject those who love you for they too are grieving with and for you.

Avoid blame and guilt... they are the poisons of the soul, powerless to return our loved ones to us. They encourage fear and harm others.

Remember the children, especially the little ones, for they are often confused and frightened.

Spend time in nature with animals, nature's greatest healers.

Spend time by the sea. Smell fresh flowers. Take long walks. Write of your pain...

Cry again...

Remember... those who you love are at peace. Rest your tired soul knowing this. They are counting on you.

For You

I wish for you that your precious heart breaks open, that all the thorns fall at your feet...

I wish for you that your fantasies crumble, your illusions be exposed, that your disappointments shatter...

I wish that you will come to know that you are stronger than you can possibly imagine.

I wish that the light of your sacredness reveals this truth to you, that the shadows of your mind dissolve into ashes leaving only that which is pure and true.

I wish for you that you take refuge in the strength and wisdom of your own inner heart, that the mystery of your divine soul be your guide... that love be your light in the darkness.

I wish for you to fall into the arms of the unknown, letting go of all your sorrows and fears, knowing the Love of the Beloved is with you always, ever carrying you.

I wish you to know that you are precious, sacred and free.

This I wish for all of you.

*

We have never been asked to be perfect. Those are the thoughts and demands of others.

Perfection is self-serving. It is never inclusive and it is a form of vanity. A spiritual greed, its pursuit always causes suffering...

Our imperfections have been given to us as teachers and guides.

Our imperfections place us on a sacred path, a journey that teaches us to love fully despite our scars and worn edges. It teaches us to forgive others including ourselves, to come to understand compassion, for we too have known great sorrow and heartbreak.

It helps us explore the gift of life given to us, the gift of being human, by doing the best we can.

No excuses, no complaints... It shows us how extraordinary our imperfections are.

What more can be asked of any soul?

*

Accept that your heart has been broken. Healing begins there.

It is in this acceptance that the light of grace enters.

Rest well.

*

"I know how you feel."

You cannot ask another to understand "how" you feel...

Nor can you understand "how" they feel...

You can identify with them. Discuss it, relate to them or empathize with them... be compassionate with them...

But you can never know "how they feel."

It is a lesson for that soul alone and no other.

*

Do not be so quick to hide from your sorrow. Within it contains the gift of healing.

*

When all that you know has been taken...

When the eye of the storm has crossed your path...

When darkness has hidden the face of the sun...

Seek the heart of love of compassion and they will come to hold you close. This too shall pass.

*

Searching

You cannot understand how to fall in love. It is not a learned experience, something taught in books or by watching others.

It is a spontaneous "knowing" at the deepest level of your being. It flows and moves freely with no effort, no controls and no gimmicks...

It is pure within itself.

Only love can recognize love.

It is the same with "spiritual presence." It is not something you ponder, seek another's point of view for, control, fabricate or hope is true. When you have had a genuine experience, you will come to see this on the most intimate level of your being...

It will not shift, leave, change or fail you, nor would it seek validation through others.

You will have no doubts.

It is recognition on the most sacred level within you. It is only then that all searching has ended.

*

When sorrow arises, those of good heart will hear its cry. They will offer themselves without a thought. They do not notice the clock, sighing with impatience...

They bring the healing touch that only Love can offer...

And they do this without asking anything in return... except your friendship.

*

Lack of self-forgiveness implies the expectation of perfection.

When perfection fails... guilt, blame and accusation come to the front.

Embrace your humanity. If you could have acted differently you would have. If you could have thought differently you would have.

This is why forgiveness is the greatest gift. It comes with its eternal twin...

Love.

*

If you need to, have a good cry...

You will feel better.

*

Please remember you are responsible for the effort, not the outcome.

If you have truly done your best, with no excuses or blame, then what more can you ask?

Hold your head high, offer thanks... and carry on.

Bring this sense of peace to your own soul.

*

Happiness is a temporary state of consciousness triggered by an event, experience or person...

Happiness is very fleeting. When it has passed we are then left unhappy, living by comparison to the past or waiting for the next happy moment. We try to create another happy experience just to keep the "high" going. We will do anything to keep happiness alive.

And so the hamster wheel keeps on spinning...

What is really sought is peace and serenity... a sense of ease.

What will bring you to this...?

*

For those who have fallen deeply in love... there is only one way to live.

For those who have fallen deeply in love... there is only one way to die.

I would not have it any other way.

*

Letting go is not something that you consciously do...

Forgetting, suppression, distraction, clever avoidance, relocation of physical space, creating artificial senses of belief and spiritual make believe places of the heart...

So many think if they use these techniques that suffering will be minimized. This is not letting go... These are forms of self-hypnosis and self-injected desire. They try to dilute the pain... and for that purpose it offers limited remedy.

It is a band aid on a sucking chest wound.

If one "tries" to let go... it becomes a tug of war. To let go or not let go... The use of will power is an internal demand that can work in the short term, but it never lasts. In the private places of the soul one can feel that they have private chains that still bind them...

So then... how then does one let go?

*

There are those who are content seeking and wishing for love.

Do not be one of those. Let go completely and fall into love's embrace.

*

How easy it is to judge another. It only takes a moment to cast another into darkness.

Understanding takes time, patience and compassion. It takes an open heart to see that very good people can sometimes make very bad choices.

47

Be careful of who you judge...

*

When you walk, walk from within.
Never walk the way fear tells you to move.

*

Love is the answer... no matter what the challenge, no matter what the heartbreak.

*

So much exhaustion from efforts of the past, so much anxiety trying to control the outcomes of tomorrow...

Have you not seen the suffering it brings to you and those you love?

Enough!

*

A blank canvas is in front of you...

Speak from your heart and write the words that you need to hear.

Write on your canvas the healing message your soul has been waiting for. Answer the inner whisper that has been calling to you...

Sit. Relax. Write...

*

Love is not written on paper. Paper burns in the fires of the world.

Love is not etched into the face of marble. Marble can crumble, the winds of time reducing it to sand.

Love is written deep within the heart... where it remains an eternal light.

*

Love cannot be held onto, controlled or manipulated.

It is a manifestation of the soul. It appears on the horizon of the heart and illuminates one's very essence. Once love has been experienced it will forever remain with you regardless of the form it takes.

No matter the time or distance. Those you love will be at peace with you.

*

Grief can make you very vulnerable... be careful who you expose it to.

*

Stand tall... Turn your face into the wind of your days. Renew the courage that flows through you.

You have been given this life with all its challenges and joys. Find gratitude in the smallest of things...

Keep it simple... Rest often... Love deeply.

Be of good will and of good heart.

Compassion is not the sign of weakness or insecurity... It is the living expression of courage.

It is a call of inner strength to put the needs of those less fortunate ahead of your own if even for a moment... to clasp hands when the rain in our lives has driven all of us to find shelter.

On behalf of those unable to say it... Thank you.

*

Where to go from here?

When your heart is broken?

When you have fallen off the edge of the world?

When all you see is darkness in the sunlight of the day, when the voices and thoughts of what was have brought you to your knees?

Where do you go from here...?

Peace to you in your ongoing recovery.

*

If you fall in love with the idea of being in love, you will find that you are romanticizing an idea... and you will begin looking for someone to complete the fantasy.

Like any movie or well written book, you will come to see it as fiction, the imaginative work of men and women. And surely within it heartbreak will follow as the book's final chapter comes to its end or the movie theater of the mind closes its doors.

What to do...?

*

I cannot think of one thing Love does not improve...

I cannot think of one thing Hate helps to heal.

*

Grief is not just the loss of a loved one.

It is a shift within your very soul.

It is a movement from being complete to being fragmented...

It brings us to our knees...

But it reminds us that only Love really matters.

*

It has been said that your heart must be broken many times before it is opened...

Mine is wide open.

*

Wake up from the dream of death and release the sorrow behind your eyes.

Let the thorns fall from your heart.

We are with you always...

We have come to sing our song.

*

Pain and suffering cracks open the soul's covering... as light always penetrates darkness.

If you must endure grief, do it well. Allow it to be and feel it all.

It is only then that your soul will be freed from the darkness of sorrow, giving way to the divine light of peace.

*

The weight of the world was never meant to be carried by only two hands.

*

Unacceptable

Can you accept that you cannot accept?

That you remain wounded and broken?

That you are angry that your prayers have not been answered?

That your feelings of hope and inner trust have been shattered? That there is no turning back?

That, despite being a decent, good person, a great suffering has been laid at your feet?

Can you look directly into the face of the Heavens and say...

"I have trouble forgiving. I am heartbroken. I have been let down. I feel so helpless... I feel I have been fooled by all who I have trusted.

What has happened to me and my family is not acceptable.

This is me. I am hurting. I am angry. It is who I am..."

The voice of your soul has spoken a great truth. No hiding, no nonsense, no acting or pretending...

No spiritual band aids.

It takes great courage to do that.

I admire you greatly. Thank you.

*

Are you willing?

Are you willing to sit with someone who has been broken by grief... and not try to fix them?

Are you willing to be present with the lonely... offering them only your quiet compassion?

Are you willing to hold the hand of someone who is lost in fear... not trying to be the expert, healer or spiritual teacher?

Are you willing to just listen to the cries of a trembling heart?

Are you willing to enter the furnace with them and give all you have?

Are you willing to stand by them just as they are, your soul meeting theirs at the center of the tightrope?

Are you willing to bear it all... for their sake?

*

Abandonment

For many, they live with a sense of being abandoned, a painful edge cutting through their soul...

A sense of abandonment may rise through one's parents, family, the rejection of a lover, the death of a child, a partner or sibling, the loss of one's career, the loss of health, the forecast of terminal illness, the loss of property and wealth, crushed hopes and dreams, the loss of one's faith...

If the wound of abandonment is still bleeding, if the wound has scarred you... what then is the healing for such a wound or injury?

The answer always lies within you.

You can never abandon your true soul, the light that is within you.

You will come to see that self-love will help you gather up the broken pieces, to hold them as a mother would hold her sick child, nurturing and healing her little one back to health...

It is through the radiance of self-love that abandonment heals.

*

May you love so completely that even the heavens will take notice.

May your love be so complete that when it is time for your departure the angels will come to gather your soul and honor your great love, like fresh rain falling upon the earth, bringing hope to those who only know the barren desert of sorrow...

*

Dying

Please stand beside me. That is all I ask.

I do not want your advice or counsel. I do not want your pity. Please do not pretend to be other than yourself with me. I understand that you are fearful, frightened and confused. I too know those feelings...

Just come and hold my trembling hand. Be present with me. Please give me all of yourself as I am giving you all of me.

If you are ashamed or embarrassed...

If you do not know what to say...

It is fine. It is the presence of your soul that brings me comfort.

As you watch me lay dying, you too are dying with me. You are dying to what was, to what might have been...

What you mourn are the dreams of the future, the fleeting images of the past... Let it all slip away. Let it fall behind the curtain of your sorrow. Join me now in the presence of this moment. It is only here that we can stand in the fire of our great love.

Come hold my hand and be my witness...

*

When you are still, the presence of your loved ones will awaken the peace within you...

The tears you cry that fall upon their hair, their smiling faces...

You will hear their laughter as they play at your side. You will hear their voice... and they will say worry not...

"I am with you... I will never leave you."

*

Fight poverty.

There is a great poverty amongst us.

The poverty of compassion, of forgiveness, of tolerance, acceptance, true love, concern, generosity, offering, giving, patience, family, faith and of each other...

Fight poverty.

*

Before you do anything else...

Say, "I love you."

You never know if you will have the chance again.

*

Being thankful is not found in the admiration of what you own or possess...

It is found in the offering of one's heart completely to another, the acceptance of them as you ask the acceptance of you...

Through all the tears, the laughter, the sorrow and joy... to be truly thankful we must embrace all of it.

Hold it close to our soul. Welcome it into our heart... for whatever has taken place it is part of the fabric of our life. These are the journeys of our souls.

Thanksgiving is found in the fall of every raindrop and every tear. It is found in the laughter of children and the embrace of two knowing love completely...

*

For all of us...

Let us close our eyes. Be still and open our hearts.

They will come to tell us of their peace, their love... they will dry our tears and kiss us to sleep.

*

Where there is sorrow, let me bring comfort.

Where there is fear, let me bring peace.

Where there is heartbreak... let me bring the light of healing.

*

As long as you seek another to make yourself whole...

As long as you seek a role, a personal drama to complete you...

As long as you seek an event, a location, substance, fantasy or teacher...

You will remain forever in the grasp of being incomplete and unrealized. A sense of less will always cling to you like a fading tattoo. You will ever need the outside to complete the inside...

It is only when the pain of being incomplete becomes unbearable that you can then stand in the honesty of your own soul and take a full accounting of yourself.

Take an unflinching look, one courageous in the passion of your heart, and peer fully into what you are, what you are becoming and what you won't let go of...

It is then that you will come to know your birthright... It is the deep freedom that lies within you. Only then can you fully embrace this gift of life you have been given, the sacredness you truly are.

Peace on your journey.

*

You never know when the moment of readiness has risen within...
Be ready to hear that which only silence can speak.

*

Rock bottom is sometimes a necessary place to build from.
Forgive yourself and move on.

*

The Secret of Oz

It was neither Dorothy's ruby red slippers nor the awe of the Great and Powerful Oz that set Dorothy free to "go home."

It was her great love of family, her devotion to friends, her willingness to help those less fortunate.

It was her courage to face her fears, to destroy evil, to hold the love of animals near to her heart.

It was her capacity to endure great loss, to surrender completely to her life's journey...

To come to know that the peace she was seeking was already within her, already given to her...

All she had to do was allow it to be...

"There is no place like home..."

Home is where the heart is... I'll meet you there.

*

Why do you weep?

Rest your heart and have no fear... The souls of your loved ones are returning home, like children hearing their mother's calling...

Love awaits them... rejoice and be happy.

*

If your forgiveness does not include you it is incomplete.

*

The happiness of the drop... is to die in the river.
The happiness of the soul... is to die in the arms of Love.

*

Don't let other people's noise drown out the beautiful song of your soul.

*

Tears are the silent messengers of your soul. They are the unheard voice of your sorrow.
Tears help to clean your wounds, to comfort your broken heart...
They are the sacred offering of your great love.

*

May the rising sun bring you hope.
May the setting sun bring you peace.
Stay alert... there are miracles happening within you.

The
Worldly

My Work
My Experiences
My Family
Recognitions

My Work

I sat with a beautiful young woman the other evening and had a conversation.

Her eyes sparkled with light and her body swayed with excitement... She chose her words very carefully, telling me of her hopes and dreams. She wanted to be married one day and have a family of her own.

Her hands drew me towards her. I reached out and offered her mine. She firmly accepted. Holding tightly we spoke about the loss of her sister, her best friend and constant companion.

I could feel her grip grow tighter and see tears welling up in her eyes.

I just listened... to her heartbreak, her courage.

A woman approached and introduced herself as her mother. She started to thank me for taking the time to speak with her daughter. Looking into her eyes as we spoke, not looking away... her mother said so few people approach her.

Her kind words surprised me.

"Your daughter is beautiful, loving, and intelligent," I told her, "and she misses her sister very much."

The mother thanked me and they said goodbye.

I heard the quiet hum of her daughter's wheelchair moving into the night and I watched this beautiful young girl born with Cerebral Palsy move with grace and dignity, struggling to keep her head erect and her hands still, tears of love for her sister captured in the corners of her eyes.

Her name was Lisa.

And she has left me a better man by allowing me to witness her great courage despite her great sorrow.

*

A young man shared with me that his heart was very heavy. Grief poured out of him. His time with his girlfriend had come to an end and he not only felt lonely and rejected, but he had discovered that she was in fact with another.

This drove an intense pain into his soul.

"I cannot accept this," he told me.

He felt lost without her and he burned to do anything he could to get her attention and affection back.

I asked him if he loved her.

"Of course I do," he said.

"Then do nothing... and let her be."

He couldn't believe my words.

"I came to see you for a way to get her back and you tell me do nothing!"

He left.

A few weeks later he called, very upset. He said everything he had been trying did not work. He was still heartbroken.

"What should I do?" He pleaded.

"Do nothing," I repeated. Nothing.

A few days ago, we met again. This time he was very calm and relaxed. He seemed happy.

"How is your girlfriend?"

"Ohhh," he began, "that's over!"

"Why is that?"

"I came to know that it was more about what I wanted, about feeling rejected, than the relationship itself," he said. "Now I am free to meet someone new if it the chance comes."

"By doing nothing, not a thing, you were forced into freedom. Through your tears, you were finding *yourself*. By not trying to stop the hurting, by allowing it to be, you released control of your demands. Behind it peace and freedom were waiting."

"Please," I asked him, "do not force yourself to meet others or find others or maneuver others for self-wanting, demand others to satisfy your wants.

Rather...

Do nothing... and meet your true self, your radiant self. Keep good company with yourself. Be self-accepting. Be self-compassionate and the universe will reveal to you her great secrets."

I watched this young man leave our meeting, disappearing into the rain...

I could almost swear that I heard him laugh as he stopped and felt the drops on his face.

*

It was early afternoon. A light rain washed away the remains of the morning. The air, cool, touched my face like a private kiss. I heard a tap on my office door almost too quiet to notice...

It's a sound I know too well.

I opened my door... one offering itself to agony and heartbreak, one adorned with a sign only those suffering can see...

No Exit. No Way Out.

In the soft pale glow of the hallway light stood a husband and wife. Two parents entered holding a day pass from the bottomless pit of the soul, where the sky is dark with fear and time offers no comfort. The father's eyes were red with sorrow, his tired arms holding up his wife as though she were wet paper... folding, collapsing under the slightest touch.

I welcomed them quiet and respectfully... Their anguish was so powerful, as if they had traveled barefoot on a road paved with broken glass and sharpened stones...

I asked them to be seated, my heart pleading with the "Father" to help me, to bring comfort to these young people, their wedding bands still new with hope and dreams...

I asked for guidance to help them push away the branding irons pressed into their soul... to help me break the chains of hell binding their wrists.

I watched them and listened. I watched as the voices of the unseen tormentors of their hearts whispered in their ears in the tongue of jackals, offering them no rest.

All they heard was the axman grinding his blade, his face hidden under the darkest cowl, where all cowards of the soul live...

They looked to me, my focus intent. My heart broke quietly.

The husband held his bride's hand, she held his hand tightly, silently pleading for him not to let go, not to let her fall back into the abyss... where the thorns are deep with red stains and the scent of despair snaps the head back like a master's whip...

I leaned forward and we began.

*

I meet so many families deeply wounded by the darkness of suicide and the fear, the guilt, frustration, anger and myriad other emotions left in its wake.

There is unbearable sorrow in not being able to recognize the wounds harming their loved ones.

There is great anguish in seeing the infection and being unable to stop its spread.

To watch a loved one fall forever into the abyss is heartbreaking.

Darkness can interrupt the life of anyone at any time. None of us are immune to its great power.

Never judge anyone who has fallen... for they too are someone's child, friend or family.

You can never measure what they have endured, the suffering that pulled at their heart's center.

Offer compassion to those who have suffered this devastating loss.

Be patient with them. Listen carefully and closely. Cry with them, hold them and allow them to express their emotions and feelings of helplessness.

They need your presence... your love.

Remember... Each beautiful soul has its divine purpose. They sought peace just like you and I...

These wounded souls found the only doorway they could. Never let their deaths be in vain.

Love them again and again.

*

I pushed away from desk, that old familiar knock drawing me to the door. My hand found the cool door knob, turned and beyond the threshold stood a young woman, perhaps in her mid-forties. Her face smiled a way I have seen too often... one driven by the unbearable, created to distract the peering eyes of the world.

Welcoming her inside, I directed her to sit and try to relax... In my soul I knew it was an impossible request.

Her suffering eyes were two dark wounds with their edges raw.

She gently placed down her cell phone. With a touch of her finger, a single red eye staring back, the digital screen popped up. All would come out with time...

I remained still for a moment. Nothing moved. Perhaps her husband, her sister, mother? I never know. Cars passed outside. A quiet rhythm of footsteps paced across the hall. The wind moved through the window as if sending a silent prayer.

He came to me slowly. His age was of 17 years. He showed me his loves, how the touch of palette and brush brought him joy. Lyrics and chords the other twin in his world of passion...

"Yes," his mother nodded. "He was an art student and musician. He wrote music, played from his heart..." Her tears ripped holes through her broken soul.

He spoke of the spider webs that gummed inside his head, the uneasy shadows that flooded his thoughts. No drugs, no alcohol for this young man... but an inner, relentless demon stayed, wearing him down.

A sudden depression rose and drove him deeper. His journey ended with a belt looped around his neck, his bedroom a private point of departure. His brother's arms found him at the chin-up bar, an unwanted partner in this handsome child's final moments.

His mother just stared at me.

"Oh my God. That is exactly what happened... how? How?"

I remained quiet. Her eyes left mine.

I watched this mother scream, pleading to wake from this nightmare. She begged for mercy, her hands grasping at her hair. She strained like an animal caught in a steel trap, its tormented cries unending, the smell of death and grief filling her senses...

I kept my eyes on her. My soul peered even more deeply. Her tears subsided for a minute. Even heavy rains go quiet for a time.

"Have you ever seen Lord of the Rings?"

She stared at me.

"Why do you ask...?"

"He's telling me that he loved that movie, especially the hobbits."

Her head began to shake.

"Are you kidding me?"

"No," I said. "He wants me to talk about the One Ring."

Her hand moved from her lap to her chest, slowly pulling out a long chain. At the end was an exact replica of the One Ring, her son's favorite.

We both sat in awe. Her son's rising soul called to his mother... his search for inner peace coming to an end. Her chest still heaving, her cries still coming, she took my hand.

"Please tell me he is alright..."

My eyes told her the truth. She knew. He had been healed... his darkness was over. His peace shined anew like a sacred light.

We took a few moments. She wanted to stay, but the world was calling for her. Finally she exhaled.

"Thank you. Thank you..."

She walked down the hallway, her face turning to the morning sun. I could hear her son singing tales of the Shire and Bilbo Baggins, of dragons and dwarves, her son's love touching the ring hanging around his mother's heart.

His soft hands drying her tears... a gentle smile came to her face.

I never witness greater sorrow than in the loss of a child...

*

The thick hot air choked my office, catching my breath off guard. Humidity drove the heat like a racehorse waiting for the final turn. A flick of my thumb and the hum of the air conditioner kicked on. Demonstrating its muscle, the cooled air drove the heat back like a well-trained athlete.

Through the air I heard it, a sound of tired legs and Velcro tied shoes. He and his wife entered the room, treading slowly, cautiously to find their seats...

I studied them briefly, the two adorned in comfortable clothing. For him an unnecessary tie and a clean white shirt, one glowing from the dry cleaners' press. His wife, his bride, was graced by a soft blue blouse. Violet flowers lie quietly. A garden scent, a rose perfume, garnished the air.

We spent a few moments in quiet. The couple tried to adjust to the impossible... rereading their "travel brochures" that point to a journey, one to be taken past time and space... an excursion to the other side of the veil, where the starting point is at the end. Their bags packed, their tape recorder in hand, a brief moment of prayer preceded...

I began to navigate this vessel across the waters of sorrow and despair, past the grave markers and glowing lighthouses...

A soul's lantern leads the way across the ocean of tears and wet handkerchiefs, bringing them to shore where peace and rest guide them home.

The contact came suddenly, not building as it often does. The collapse, the starvation, the gaunt stare of a dying man... a man among men...

It stood before me.

I felt a "hot iron bubble" rise in my chest...

I could not get rid of it. I could not swallow it... nor spit it out.

I looked directly in his eyes. His wife held his arm, the gentlest touch, one tender to his heartbreak.

The soul I was seeing died at the hands of his abusers, his tormentors. They fed him dysentery. They offered him malaria as a house guest. Their bamboo poles were play toys on his broken limbs, the laughter of hyenas his lullaby.

This young American, a pilot, spent his final days in a violent hotel in the north of Vietnam... Hanoi, where hell took session, was a classroom where cruelty and torture were chalked on the board...

He died among the smell of duck feces and stale water. He died starving. He died in a shallow grave without his name, without his family. He died among his brothers, their gaunt stares opening the trapdoor.

Tears flushed the eyes of my guests. The husband and wife, held on, their eyes closed...

I shared then this final piece of his story.

He told me he was their son.

That when he died he lifted his arm, one that had been broken by the steel fist of his keepers, an arm that had remained deformed and shattered...

...because they found him saluting.

Made from his pants cloth and colored by his own suffering... he saluted to an American flag, one he had kept hidden in his mud cell only to be discovered by the eyes of hate.

The parents stared in amazement. A young Navy pilot, his soul now at rest, found his parents on the eve of our Independence Day.

May this hero continue to rest in peace.

*

One evening I was working in a local eatery. The tables were full and the clamor of conversation rolled in and out like the ocean dancing to the music of a full moon...

Waiters and busboys flew about effortlessly as if in thrall to their queen bee. The bartender leaned at his castle measuring the patrons with a seasoned eye and welcoming smile, all the while controlling the game.

The evening starts. Infused with Spirit, my work began.

The readings were beautiful and intense. The agony of broken hearts, but also the healing and the love of families finding their ways back home... across the broken bridges of time, reuniting in the embrace of love letters sent through the ether.

A child finding its mother. A husband once again holding his wife. A sister reuniting with her twin.

Grief falls on the floor. Smiles and sobs arise like balloons of white light, those smiles now illuminating the room brighter than candlelight...

I was drawn to one young man in particular. Sitting with his family and friends, his arms were folded and his lips stiff. He looked firm in a fighter's way with a dockworker's glare.

His eyes were those that had seen too much and could forget very little.

I saw the squint in his eyes, the large doubts in his grin... gestures of a cynic, the mimic of one trying to uncover the magician.

Then I saw the explosion.

The Humvee reduced to scrap metal. An erupting inferno, one only Dante himself could have witnessed. Metal flying like splinters into the night, like angry hornets piercing the body, removing the face... leaving the remains of an American child in a land of sand and hell...

The soul of an American hero had found his brother in arms on a quiet road in a restaurant thousands of miles away.

A hero returned home past the desert, past the heartbreak that litters the runways and came home... his body left in the embers, his soul marching in cadence to the Halls of Montezuma.

The guest at the table looked at me, tears in his Marine Corps eyes. The Red and Gold warrior lowered his head in a private moment. The red, white, and blue glowed of Old Glory rested her hand on his back.

He looked at me in disbelief... The Marine had come to undo me, to unravel the evening.

But those eyes born in Semper Fidelis could not find the source of the magician's illusion... for there was nothing to be found.

"How?" He asked. "How could you have known? I don't know you. I've never met you! He was my best friend... My brother in arms!"

I did not move as he gathered himself, reclaiming his focus and trying to shake off what he thought impossible...

I stood silently. The grief, the joy, the disbelief all came together... The Marine's family was quiet, allowing him to take it all in...

I reached across the table and, looking directly into his eyes, extended my hand... He took it.

"Thank you for your service. It's been an honor to meet you."

I held his gaze and felt his grip. For that moment, in silence, all was said. I then asked the audience to join me in applause, to thank him.

I moved on to the next table and to the next. Soon the night came to a close, with darkness demanding an exit.

As I left I saw a glint of metal and heard the sound of an uneven step. It was the young Marine, his artificial limb a constant companion... a souvenir from Hell.

Laughter peppering his voice, he wore a smile that would capture any young girl's heart. Inside I clapped for him, my heart bursting in pride.

As he walked to his waiting ride, I looked closely. At times a shadow, moving in and out of my sight, carried the colors of the Marine Corps aside his friend, his brother. All is well, it seemed to whisper. And then, as he came to me, so did he return across the veil, his death one of valor.

For the Marine at the table, I knew he would never forget his friend. It was finding him again, needing to say good bye. Unable to put his helmet on his rifle, unable to locate his tags... that haunted him.

Never leaving a man behind... that brought him to the evening.

And now, on a quiet night on Long Island, at a table of family and friends... two Marines found each other again.

They stood side by side, the soul of one celebrating the life of the other.

A helmet was finally in place, a folded flag at home and a grateful prayer finally spoken.

My Experiences

It was early morning and the leaves on the trees stretched to the sun, offering gratitude for its warmth.

The still pond waited to receive its daily guests. With beautiful white feathers and rainbow collars, elegant ducks and swans sprinkled the water. Lovely voices called to each other, each allowing the other to move easily and quietly through the lily pads, finding purchase among fallen birch trees that lay like broken statues across the mouth of the pond.

And then, as I walked... I saw the eyes, eyes that bore bright through the underbrush. Looking again, I saw they were gone.

As first I thought I had been mistaken. Perhaps the sunlight caught a reflection. I pressed onward through the dried sticks, the moss and the trees lining the path like an old covered bridge.

As I came back past that same place I saw the eyes again and this time I was going to find out what it was...

And find out I did.

A charming young rabbit had found a place to rest!

I approached quietly, asking permission to enter, expecting him to run.

But he did not.

And as I grew closer and knelt down, I saw it.

His rear legs had been broken, his little torso twisted...

His eyes pleaded for help.

I took off my shirt and gently wrapped him in it. I kept talking to him, a tear in my eye, telling him no one else would hurt him. He must have understood, as I felt him relax.

I drove him to my friend's veterinary office, some 30 minutes away. He lay down, quietly suffering. My heart was breaking for this little soul.

My friend met me at the door of his office.

This little one had to be put down, he said. It had broken its back.

I turned away and said a quiet prayer. It was an honor for me to be with this scared, little soul, now One in spirit.

You never know when your presence might be asked.

I found myself humbled and grateful for this adorable little one, who brought a man to his knees to say a prayer...

To say goodbye.

*

My Own Truth

How often I would find myself defensive, wearing the mask for others and using anger and defiance as a hammer and nail.

How I would slip in and out of self-honesty, taking the back door to avoid self-scrutiny, blaming my past, my parents, friends or family for my short comings or difficulties.

I'd look to run and hide in the fantasy of my own thoughts as a human turtle, its head well hidden within the shell, and no matter how clever I was or no matter how slick I became, I would always wake up next to myself, disconnected and in great pain.

Once again I would look for the trapdoor, a new costume, ever arguing the case for self-deception.

How fortunate I was.

*

I saw a beautiful little boy, no older than three, dragging an adult size garden rake along his front lawn. His smile was wide and his chest full of pride. His father was nearby, busy gardening.

The wind moved across their faces. The dad turned, reached and lifted his son high, kissing his face and holding him close. Two or three seconds of magic that words could not describe... and then he carefully placed the boy back down.

Together they became One, enjoying the smell of fresh earth, the spring air in their lungs... his little hands safe within his dad's warmth.

Silence smiled as I saw dad and son enjoying the simplicity of pulling a garden rake over a lawn, each blade of grass playing tag... They were catching sunlight in their hands, the scent of new life filling their noses....

I watched as the birds applauded what they saw, their feathers serving their hidden purpose. I saw squirrels dancing in time to the heartbeat of father and son. I saw the leaves of spring bowing in approval of their love.

How awesome to witness the innocence of pure joy.

*

I went to my local deli one morning. The line was long, the coffee hot and in high demand.

"You're up next, Mike," a counter worker called out. No one seemed to move. No hands waved, no voices responded.

Standing behind me was a young man carefully unfolding his dollar bills. His stature short, his face slightly wide wearing glasses thick, he had a slight pull to his eyes.

"Are you Mike...?" I asked him.

"Yes," he said, his head lowering slightly, concentrating deeply.

"I think you're next."

"All right," he said. My hand guided him to the head of the line...

I watched him extend a few dollar bills. The kind worker smiled.

"Here ya go, Mike. Thanks!"

Handing him his change and a paper bag full of breakfast fare, Mike waved his hand. The deli man returned the gesture...

Mike paused. His left hand clutching the bag, right one placing ear plugs under his ski hat, his iPod ready, a travel companion...

I watched him disappear into the day's bright cold. He seemed to be moving to his own inner voice, inward personal reminders ringing for handling the realm of strangers and the unfamiliar...

I felt my heart smile. I crossed paths with this young man with Down syndrome, my soul grateful for the moment. Glad I was to be in the presence of this silent teacher of the heart, one telling all who would listen that his place was as precious, important and sacred as anyone else... one teaching that life is to be lived and enjoyed no matter its struggles and challenges, that we are all born of the same Creator, each unique and loved completely...

How beautiful to witness.

Thank you Michael. I wish you peace always.

*

Tiny Feet

I walked into my local supermarket this morning, an electric eye winking at me and two large doors sliding apart... I felt like Moses for just a second. Air conditioning snapped my skin and the aroma of produce and fresh vegetables turned my head... Nearby a small counter display of fresh cut flowers wrapped in cellophane waited for a new home...

I strolled down an aisle. A poster of a karate kid with a big smile stared grabbed my eyes... Got some ice cold milk, some boxes of cereal, fresh chicken off the grill and more knick-knacks...

As I stood in line, the cashiers busy before me, my eyes caught a look at the magazines... Divorce and infidelity... Too much money, too little money... Glossy people with glossy problems... Another turn of the wheel and so it goes.

One aisle over I saw a grandmother and her granddaughter at her side, the baby perhaps two years old... Her sun suit and sandals were fresh with summer's warmth. Her tiny arms swung in the air playing with her private angels... the safety of her stroller and her grandmother's love all she needed.

I paused just to take it in, everything else melting away.

"I love you," the grandmother said, her head bending forward. The baby wrapped her arms around her neck.

"Give me a big kiss," grandmother asked. The baby reached up like a tiny bird, her little face happy and bright with joy... her tiny lips wetting her grandma's face, her tiny hands holding the soft skin of her aging cheeks.

"I love you," the baby said, her tiny feet kicking the air.

"I love you too," said the grandma, a love in her voice sung straight from the heart.

How beautiful to witness on this summer morning, a gift freely given standing on a checkout line... The presence of innocence filling my soul...

*

There are many who have fallen into the dark places of the world. They have taken up residence within the empty corners of their minds, where thorns and broken glass have their way...

They often seek escape through self-harm, self-destruction... They cannot protect themselves from their own choices...

There is a terrible misunderstanding that somehow, through the effort of will or threats, they can just stop.

They cannot.

It is as if a madman tried to free a madman.

Take every step necessary to lead them to recovery. Never give up. Never.

There are miracles within every breath and every moment. Do what must be done. They are counting on you. Even though they struggle to ask for help, do it. No matter how many times they let you down, keep fighting.

Remember the times when they were free and happy...

Help guide them home.

I know it all... I was one of them.

28 years sober. By God's grace we go.

*

My wife and I went out to take care of some errands. My frame relaxed, I sat in the passenger's seat, our SUV a workhorse for the family.

NFL football talk on the wire, a cup of hot coffee sat in the arm rest... All being well, our conversation was one about the kids, plans for the upcoming week, questions about dinner.

We left through the backside alley of our local shopping center, a land of garbage dumpsters and debris, abandoned car tires and plastic bags. Seagulls flew overhead with free lunch on their minds. The air stung with a winter chill. My eyes glanced here and there while my wife's hand adjusted the radio...

"Stop," I yelled suddenly. "Stop the car!"

She braked. Glancing at her, I pointed it out. Raw and naked, a human foot stuck out from under a pile of garbage and old boxes.

I raced out of the SUV, my heart pounding.... I approached with caution. You never know what one may find in the dark places of the world. I looked closely... No doubt it was a foot, one completely exposed, red, raw and full of sores...

My eyes searching, I moved closer and then, as though born from the refuse, a man sat up, his left arm shielding his face from the sun...

"Are you okay?" I asked. "It's freezing."

He looked at me, his face torn by years of suffering. His teeth were uneven and decayed. Around his neck three pairs of rosary beads hung. His clothing was stained with filth.

"Where are your shoes...?"

"I don't know," he said.

"Your feet..."

"I know," he said. "I have frostbite. I can't feel them much."

My heart sank.

The scent of urine caught my nose. I reached into my pocket and pulled out some silver and paper. Handing it to him, he stared at me.

"That's $20. Get something to eat," I said.

"Thanks mister, thank you!" His eyes glistened with tears.

I called 911. In a moment red and blue lights had found him and strong hands lifted him up onto a stretcher... Those who live through the "call of the heart" took care of him...

We pulled away from the parking lot, our backseat full of groceries and warm food.

I went quiet. My thoughts and prayers plead for this shoeless stranger. I watched as a broken man disappeared into the back of an ambulance, glad to give a small gift of hope to his tired soul on this frozen winter day.

*

The Blue Haired Man

I stood waiting on line at our local supermarket where I saw a young man standing quietly by the cash register. His eyes were relaxed, his posture lean... his face seemed to say he was in his late twenties...

His hair had some blue streaks. His ears were decorated with steel hoops called gauges. His lip was pierced with a single ring. His denims were neat and his winter jacket was open and clean.

Some of the older patrons stared at him. Others spoke behind his back, while others couldn't care less, rushing to fill their shopping carts.

My line was moving quickly. I heard another patron mutter under his breath that this man looked "like a clown." That if it were up to him "he would pull out those earrings and give him a kick in the ass."

My eyes focused and my hearing sharpened as my instincts were now on edge. The line kept moving, but the man with the blue hair remained, resting at the wall. The muttering man left and started up his truck, decals of a bullseyes and spiders webs piercing his window...

Out from nowhere two teenagers came from the bread aisle. Their arms wrapped around this polite young man. Both fellows bore the traits of Down syndrome.

"You guys did great," the blue haired man said. As they smiled and gave each other high fives, I stepped forward.

"Excuse me," I said. "Do you work with these young people?"

"Yes, I live with them. They're my responsibility... they're great."

I shook his hand.

"Thanks for stepping up. Special Education is a great calling."

"Yes," he said. "I have a CSW. At night I'm in a band... I'm a drummer."

"Got it," I said. "Keep it up. It was a pleasure to meet you."

In the distance I watched them walk to their van, this blue haired man one with the affection of two young adults who only see his compassion and love in his heart.

I remained silent, the three of them humbling my soul.

*

I sat at Dunkin' Donuts, relaxed with a hot cup of coffee and the paper laid out in front of me. In the background there was a constant rhythm of customers on the move. Businessmen and women, high school teens, sanitation workers, volunteer firefighters and on and on...

I suddenly heard my name. Looking up, I saw standing there an old acquaintance. His face was empty and his eyes seemed to jump about as if searching for someone.

"It's good to see you," I said. "Please sit down."

"I've seen you in public a few times, at restaurants and theaters."

"Thanks," I said. "I hope you enjoyed it.

"I did... I just never approached you before."

"Never a problem... How can I help you?"

His head dropped and his eyes shifted away from mine.

"My sister died last year... She was only two years older than me. We were very close. I just can't get past it... I cry all the time. I don't want to work... She was like my Mom. She helped raise me... Our real mother died when I was very young..."

I sat and listened, just lending a compassionate ear.

"I am seeing a therapist," he said finally. "And they want to help me find 'closure.' Closure? How the hell do I find closure?"

His face fell into his hands.

"I am heartbroken..."

How would you comfort him?

Closure is never complete, nor should it be.

True love always carries the price of great grief.

It is not a defect.

It is the truth of the soul.

*

Cancer

The rain pounding the sidewalk, I had just entered my local supermarket. My old work boots held their own.

I grabbed some Italian Bread, a fresh rotisserie chicken, some grapes and another half-gallon of milk. The line short, I rushed up. My hair still wet, I wiped my hands off on my jeans.

At the register stood a middle aged woman I see from time to time. She is normally quiet and polite, her patient manner one of a person who has spent most of her life in the retail trade.

Today there was a noticeable glow in her face. Her smile wide, her voice carried a hidden joy...

"You look pretty happy today," I said.

"I am! I just finished my radiation and chemo," she said. "My PET scan came back clean... I am cancer free!"

My heart was full of thanks.

"That's terrific! After work you have to celebrate," I said. She nodded as she filled the shopping bags, her tired legs moving with no effort. As I began to leave she turned to me.

"Hey... enjoy every moment!"

The wind was driving hard now, bending the trees at their waists. I sat back in my car for a moment, the rain water dripping off my face.

I closed my eyes in reflection. How fortunate I was to hear this story of hope and recovery from a gentle, quiet woman, a woman granted a great pardon on this stormy day...

My Family

I remember a night some time ago…

A restless crying came from my daughter's bedroom. I checked the hour and knew she had been sleeping for some time. From that deep sleep an unsettling restlessness had taken her over. She was having a nightmare.

My daughter tossed and turned. She was suffering in her sleep.

All of my protective instincts could do nothing. I could not enter her thoughts to rescue and defend her from these imaginary enemies.

Should I allow her to continue to struggle? Or should I wake her?

Sitting quietly next to her, moving her pet teddy bear Hershey over, I gently held her. She woke and I dried her tears on my t-shirt.

"Daddy," she said. "I was so scared. I couldn't find you!"

"I am right here, sweetheart. And I did not leave you!"

Her face relaxed, sensing it was a dream. At peace, her body smiled.

We live our lives much like my daughter, in and out of good and bad dreams, feeling separated and alone.

Once we truly grasp that we are all One, truly children of the divine, we are "awakened from our deep sleep" by gentle hands that guide us all.

We discover the great peace and serenity that is our birthright.

We have been given life to be fully awake, not to live in unease and fear.

We have been given this life to be open and free.

The generous spirit of the universe is constantly trying to free us from the illusion of self. It is her gift… if only we would open it!

Hershey the Bear, ever faithful and loyal, still stands guard at her pillow after all these years.

My daughter rested her head.

"Good night," she said to Hershey... and she slept peacefully. At rest, her soul was renewed and a soft light danced above her.

Maybe it was my imagination, but Hershey seemed to be smiling!

*

I went to see my son play in a hockey game. When I arrived at the arena my heart was well placed in my throat, my eyes watching, seeking my son who would enter the rink. I had expected him to play with those of his own. Young adults, other children who discovered life through hospital doors, emergency rooms, special ed classes and small yellow buses.... but this was not to be.

Men entered the arena, fully suited in battle armor... The puck snapped, skates glided and helmets flashed by warning "don't tread on me..."

And my son...

A child of 20 years, he stepped onto the rink and the whistle sounded. The puck was dropped and I spoke my first prayer was quietly and quickly...

"Keep him safe. Let him play to his heart and try his best. Let him feel free, even if he is afraid. Be his coach. Have his back, for those who challenge him do not know, nor have not been told, my son was born with autism, and they will give him no quarter..."

They played from period to period, sticks strafing, bodies spinning, shots slapping, would-be goals blocked... and then the final buzzer.

My head holding itself up with the help of my hands, tears streaming down my face, my fist punched a hole in the air...

He won. My son's team had won the game, meeting the challenge of those hardy men.

My autistic child rose from the depths of frustration, spoke his mind and played the whole game as an equal. He shook the defeated men's hands and patted their backs. His teammates embraced him as one of their own.

He stepped over the boards and placed his arms over my neck, the ocean of my heart filling the arena. We hugged, his eyes looking into mine, his voice clear, his jersey wet.

"I'll see ya home, Dad."

We parted, my son driving his own car, calling his girlfriend, the sweat of his hockey jersey well earned.

I sat quietly in my car. I had to pull off the road. In the shadows of a tree, my breath in gulps, I prayed deeply in thanks, for I had witnessed my son become a man...

He is a man who has faced his autism, has let nothing stop him, and despite many challenges... My son, my hero... He let me witness a miracle on ice, a journey to the land of the impossible...

As I returned home I realized my son was given to me to be my teacher, my candle in the dark and my guide as well... for who really was in the dark? All those years of fear and worry...

I pulled into my driveway with a joy that I could and cannot find words to explain. I watched a young man take his girlfriend's hand and walk into the night laughing all the way... with the sound of yellow school buses far off in the distance.

All my love to my son, of whom I could not be more proud.

*

The bathtub water lay warm and still, like a welcoming liquid sandbox. Towels folded neatly keep each other's company nearby, one upon the other playing pyramid, squeezing to be first to the top...

Streams of light break through the window demanding notice, magical runways waiting for playmates created in their wakes...

Evening was upon me. The night air offered her cooling song, but the daylight had yet to rest...

My son enters, his tiny hands pushing open the door and his tiny toes gripping the cool bathroom tile as if a hockey player making company with ice...

He shed his pajamas. His protector and companion Buzz Lightyear fell to his feet like a pile of autumn leaves.

His underwear hung from him, the pale image of Spiderman making his final bow...

He climbed upon the sink, pulling at his favorite toys. His well-worn friendly dinosaur, a few Matchbox cars, a tired ball bounced one time too many...

My arms hold him tightly... balance still a skill to be learned. The innocence from accidents caused him no concern or notice. His heart song drummed him into laughter and play...

I placed my son into the tub... a private ocean to him. He immediately calls his friends to play, commanding their movements and splashing them into submission. He hugs them like family members.

The bathwater ripples like an unseen propeller driving the waves. Squirted geysers up the sidewalls, overflowing waterfalls spilling onto the floor... laughter ever the music, a pure joy of the heart...

I sat and watched my son, my heart on fire. My eyes took it all in. I opened the shampoo... the color of liquid ivory flows into my hands. A strange bouquet captures my son's attention, his sapphire eyes peeking through silver and white bubbles...

As the evening continues her dance and the Purple Dinosaur calls to my son, I pull him from the belly of his private ocean. Plop into his favorite towels he goes, his fresh pajamas soon to follow. His sense of play renews...

I hold him in my arms, his face bonding with mine. His small arms find purchase around my neck and a kiss seals the deal...

The alarm clock rings.

I shake off my sleep. My dream drifts back into my memory...

The house is busy with people now. Hair dryers buzz. A polished car in the driveway, chariot for the evening, waits.

I walk into my son's room. He wears a tuxedo... Buzz Lightyear shed long ago.

A bow tie slightly turned, a shoe lace not yet tied... I bring him the corsage for his lady in waiting, her chariot humming in expectation.

It is my son's Senior Prom, another stage nearing its end.

I place my arms over my son's shoulders, looking into the eyes of a man, my son...

My knack for having much to say fails me.

I hug him with all the strength my heart can bring. I fix his tie... and I stand beside him, ever grateful for my days.

I peak into the bathroom... and I remember.

I am his father. He is my son... I remember.

*

One morning I quietly opened the door to my daughter's bedroom. I stood at her bedside and listened to her breathe as I looked around at her stuffed animals, protectors keeping her company through the night...

I said a prayer of thanks to my daughter. I thanked her for selecting me to be her dad, with all my faults and limitations.

I prayed deeply for guidance and for limitless love to bless my daughter especially on this day, this Sweet Sixteen of hers, and I prayed that as she awakens she finds the Beloved's great presence.

I asked that she be given the gifts of compassion and silence, the touch of sunshine and the peace of wind and to know that as long as "I am," I will always be there for her.

I am her dad, forever and with all my love. I could not be more proud.

*

This morning I had some tough choices to make with two of my kids. What they had asked for was not in their best interests.

They wanted to hear Yes... They heard No.

I did not say No because I was busy, it was inconvenient, they were bothering me or that I like being a dictator.

I said No because it was a bad choice they were making. My being their father requires my responsibility in guiding them to the best of my ability.

We spoke openly and honestly, each listening to the other. At times voices rose, at others voices went quiet...

Bottom line... My decision stood. They were not very happy.

It is always easier to take the path of least resistance, to just say Yes and let them do what they want to get rid of the problem...

I usually do say Yes, because in most cases they do choose wisely. Not today. Being a parent is always life on the razor's edge... but today the answer was No.

They both called me afterward and said thank you.

I thanked them as well. It is called respect. My heart is happy for them, my soul proud of them... and I told them so.

I love being a Dad. I would not have it any other way.

*

I always tell my children...

"I love being your dad."

They roll their eyes and look at the ceiling.

"Dad," they say, "we're too old for that!"

I look in their eyes and I repeat it.

As they fall asleep at night I notice smiles at the edges of their hearts.

*

I sat down next to my father today.

My hands gently touched his face. His sleep deep, the wind whispered its music through the window. I allowed myself to listen to his breathing, wisps shallow from his chest like a newborn's.

I quietly traced along the deep blue veins on his hands, hands that fought bravely for four years in World War II, hands that guided him in the night, hands that rescued children, brought fear into criminals and comforted the weak and helpless...

The hands of a police officer... hands that held me tight when I felt most afraid.

I stepped back and wiped a tear from my face.

My dad's face is cut and bruised, his arm swollen with small wounds. He lost his grip and fell in the bathroom. These once strong hands let him down. And as he fell a piece of him remained on the bathroom floor.

It is a piece he cannot reclaim.

I carried my dad into the bedroom, wrapping his wounds and kissing his head.

To my father I offered my hands... to shower and shave him... to protect him.

He is my father. I am his son.

I held my dad's hands until he fell asleep, the wind whispering through the window.

I folded my hands in prayer and gently knelt by him, thanking him for being my dad...

His hands seemed to glow in the light of the day...

Perhaps it was more...

He is my father and I am his son.

*

Falling

I remember my dad, my hero falling into darkness. His mind was betraying him. I remember my mom being so patient, so loving with him...

I remember my brothers and me standing nearby, our hearts and hands ready and open, hugging him, kissing his tired face, fixing his pajamas and wiping the cake crumbs and spilled coffee...

"It's okay, Pop. It's okay... we are here."

I remember his eyes red with age, peering into the morning light... His mind was back in Brooklyn, the '20s his last memory...

I remember he would look at my face, his oldest son... a face so familiar but one lost to a time gone by... I remember his eyes looking into mine. No voice, no nod... as if he were living in a faraway land of strangers.

I remember my head turning away, my heart breaking and tears in my eyes.

My hero was fading.

An invisible enemy I could not fight... this adversary would give him no rest.

I remember when we found him, his thin arms laying at his side, his head leaning backward... his gentle smile captured in a private prayer...

Alzheimer's had taken his mind, his life... but not his soul. Not his love. Not his radiant heart.

They thrive deep within my chest... and these I will never lose.

*

The blood of the Norsemen ran through my father's veins. He was a Viking from the legends of Odin and his son Thor.

His tales will be told today so that at his knee the grandchildren will hear them...

The tales of a World War II veteran who braved the Atlantic and held firm his post...

The stories of the decorated police officer who ran into the inferno when others stepped aside...

His comrades and fellow seamen call from Valhalla, the hall of the great warriors...

They stand silently as the waves in the fjords smash upon the rocks.

Flaming arrows are ready to be let loose. The calling is made to one of their own. A solitary long ship, the vessel of the Nordic giants, awaits him...

Its sails call to him for his last journey...

But for this day the shadows only rise and fall. My father is at my side once again and by God's Grace I will hold him and wipe away his tears. I will place his hand with my mother, who has stood by this warrior for more than 70 years...

*

My mother reached out, her tired fingers trying to stay steady. Dark spots like tired pennies sprinkle the back of her hand. The glow of her Irish emerald ring catches the attention of the darkness. Her body, swollen by time and driven by the demands of motherhood and heartache, leans into her arm chair... A muffled sound is released, the groan of the springs pushing themselves to protect and support the one they have known for so many years...

Her chair, her guardian and constant companion seems to guide her, steadying so that no balance is lost, no dignity loosened.

She slowly finds the hand of my father. He sits quietly nearby, his bride of forever at his side.

Yet my dad's mind moves in and out of this time and place... how often his mind returns him home to the sound of the Brooklyn Dodgers and trolley cars, the iron horses that still pull his memory, to meeting my mother on the side steps of a small courthouse. There he promised his love to his Irish rose.

But the cold waves of war break over his memories... So many friends of his youth marched into Hell with him and lay themselves under the waves, taking permanent residence with Davy Jones... all before my father's heartbroken eyes.

I sat still only a few feet away, bearing witness. My, what my eyes held and my ears heard brought... bring tears. The tears one has holding a newborn... The saltwater of the soul that lies quietly waiting for those moments that come from beyond imagination, that are only born out of the magic of life, the devotion of true love...

From what seemed out of the Land of Nowhere, a moment in my father's mind seemed to release him. His eyes glowed as the jailer of his soul fell asleep while on duty...

A light pierced the darkness... and he found my mother's gaze. He placed his hand upon hers and then spoke quietly, like a loud whisper...

He asked her to marry him, to be his partner.

He did not ask in a way that one might refresh one's vows or in a private time reinforces one's heart.

He spoke in that raw innocence of a first time love.

His words came out in polished black shoes, a box of candy... a way that stops your heart and catches your breath. It brings fire into your soul.

He asked her from his heart, his mind being pushed aside by his love. The love that first brought him to the steps of the courthouse so long ago where his Irish rose was in full bloom, brilliant with all its petals glowing with hope...

I sat back in disbelief of what he said. Tears slid down my face, turning my cheeks wet and my heart into clouds.

On this quiet night my father taught me again about his love of my mother, his partner, his lifeline. He taught me he meaning of the struggle...

Of family.

My mother held my father's hand, like two tired tree roots that have been woven together by the hot sun and the driving rains that lay now in the gentle grass of the final years...

It was so beautiful, I said. My face beamed, tears staining my shirt... I ached for conversation... a resurrection of my dad's mind.

There was no response.

No answer was given.

My dad laid his head back, his mouth open like a fish seeking water. His mind again returned to the clang of the trolley cars, Duke Snider, Ebbets Field, subway tokens and of the shadows of men who searched the apartment buildings for the iceboxes and the coal bins, the sound of broken radios...

These are his personal love letters from the past.

I stood up, wiping away my disappointment, celebrating the window shade opened only to be closed too quickly once again...

I kissed my father's head and held my mother tight. As I left through the warming glow of my childhood home, I looked back...

I saw my mother kissing Santa Claus.

*

I have been taught to offer my hand first.

To acknowledge the stranger with a respectful greeting.

To hold the door open, to pull out a chair for a woman, or walk her home... and to do all of this even if no thank you is offered.

I do it for myself... for I must enjoy and be at peace with my own inner reputation. I can say without pause that I have been taught to look for the best in others... but to be quite ready for their worst.

I have been taught to be proud of my country and to honor our flag each and every day. I have been taught to thank the veterans and to honor the sacrifice they have made... to lay wreaths, wear poppies and shake their hands... to offer honest gratitude.

I have found that I feel more complete and more at rest in myself when I respect and appreciate others who have tried to improve this world, to take a stand and give it all. Whether or not they have failed I offer applause from my heart, for they have taken the road less traveled.

I have learned to bend a knee for the children and the elderly, for the sick, the dying and the children of special needs.

I have learned to look the desperate in the eye and shelter the weak and less able from the storm.

I have been taught to be the first to offer and the last to ask, and to always offer more than to expect in return.

I have been taught that family can only be first.

When I am centered and well within myself, I have been taught to pray often for what I truly need and to be careful for that which I want.

I have been taught to honor my life and yours. I have realized that those who provided these lessons, my parents, taught me without words.

They taught by their actions... and I am proud and humbled that my mother and father always lived in this way.

I am proud and honored, as their son, to have been blessed enough to call them my parents.

*

Entering my church, the echo of my steps whispered alone.

I watched the shadows and stained glass dancing in silence. There was an older woman moving from statue to statue. Her soft white hair peeked from underneath the shawl draping her head. An old school Catholic, she observed reverence in her private light... her lips kept kissing her fingers, her fingers touching the feet of each patron saint. A slow rotation, the marble floor watched her balance.

I sat in a pew, my knees folded and my head lowered. I make the sign of the cross, exhale and pray to my brother's soul.

I told him our family and friends will gather to pay their respects to him and honor his life. They will comfort his wife and children and carry our mother's broken heart across the abyss. They will share stories and laughter, tears and private moans.

The sound of grief is unmistakable.

I sat still against the hardwood and closed my eyes.

Through the corner of my soul I saw my brother's bright smile, his face glowing and relaxed. Just as quickly he was gone, a glint breaking the darkness, his soul beginning its rise to glory...

I heard the voice of our father calling to him, guiding him to the way of peace and rest that he so badly needed...

Grief is for the living. It's for us to bear not as a punishment or form of self-torture, but as a reminder of how precious and sacred we are. It tells us reunion and peace will be the path. It is to teach us that all is temporary... save for Love.

Love will never end.

This is the gift that I found in the pew of my local church today, a gift wrapped by my brother. His strong hands offered it to me with my tears falling still on the marble steps.

I bowed my head in thanks.

I love you, my brother.

*

I approached my mother's home. The driveway taken by visiting cars, I noticed through opened windows the baby seats and carry bags resting in the broken sunlight...

As I entered the residence of my youth an Irish flag danced in the breeze as though inviting me in. A dancing Leprechaun protecting his pot o' gold glanced at my arrival. The aroma of home cooking and tea kettles filled my memories.

In attendance... Mom, my brother Bill, two of my brothers-in-law Ken and Arbey, my two daughters Jesse and Kyla, my niece Jackie and her beautiful baby Brooke, only 5 months old, my granddaughter Maddy enjoying her 4 month rising, our dog Danny and our family's rescue dog Bubba all moved about...

I sat back in the chair my dad always sat in, my hands and heart holding my granddaughter Maddy, baby Brooke on deck with plenty of kisses and hugs waiting to be shared. I always fall hard for infants. They bring the light of innocence to the dark places hiding in my soul.

We gathered at the kitchen table speaking of what was and is, plates of chicken and fresh vegetables emptying quickly...

Little ones have their own timetable. Who had to change into their pajamas? Who needed to be walked and have their back gently tapped? My daughter's ear focused on her babies burps... one, then two... all is good. My head nodded in approval.

I sat quietly, my eyes moving about and I noticed my niece flinch, sadness in her eyes. Her head dropped, her one lip biting the other...

"My dad never met Brooke," she said, the love and beauty of her first child falling absent when her dad, my brother died, a vacancy clearly left in her happiness. I nodded.

"You know Daddy was there with you sweetheart, loving all of it."

"Uncle Bobby, I know that... I believe that... It's just not the same."

Her tears filled spaces once held by hope.

I looked at her, her breaking heart torn by love and grief. Exhaling softly, my frame pushed off the arm rests. I kissed her face and held her tight, my hand rubbing the back of her head.

I said nothing at all.

There are moments when words cannot heal. Only love and the truth of your soul can do it.

The hands on the wall clock demanded my attention. I waved goodbye to my family, a gesture from my soul for those who live in my heart.

I moved into the night air, my head turning briefly for just one more glance. I view the glow of Mother's home, its appearance like a warmly lit shadow box, the sound of conversations fading in the distance...

As I stepped onto the sidewalk, I stood still for a moment. I felt two old friends approaching, their presence well known to me...

Silence and darkness stood at my side, both waiting to guide my wounded heart home.

*

Tired from the day's demands, I returned to my home. The lights were muted and my children were quiet...

My daughter, the youngest one, sat on the living room floor. Her cheeks puffy, tears welled from her eyes and tap danced on her blouse. My two sons knelt, in search of their feelings. Apples caught in their throats, words proved elusive.

My wife lay on her side, her face offering her full throbbing heart, trapped in barbed wire...

Removing my shoes, I stepped into the healing, second skin of my sandals. I entered the small circle of my family, lying next to my wife. Like a well-placed bet she too held tears.

Our dog Danny, born in the blossom of spring, had returned home from his second surgery in less than a fortnight. His hips had tricked him, his body fooled by the promise of youth...

Danny Boy is my fifth child. He is my friend, companion and charge. I love him completely.

My wife brings a cool bowl of water, an elixir speckled by ice chips. Surrounded by his favorite toys, he lies on top of his blanket, one worn well at the edges. My old gym shirt rests only inches from his nose, that in my absence I will be there...

We are his family and we offer him his favorite meal... Hugs, kisses... A gentle hand.

His eyes have a shrouded glow... for the morphine still has its way with him. His head lies heavy. His moist nose drifts uninterested from his food.

He tears at his bandages, confused by their scent. Wrappings around his legs, his shaved hindquarters catch my eye, forcing me to look away.

But my eyes always return... and I offer him my touch.

I say a private prayer to give my Danny the grace of healing and the peace of acceptance.

Danny will heal well. The hands of the surgeon played their gentle guitar in healing my son, restoring him to where he began before this shift.

As a family we will take care of one of our own, without pause or excuse, without pointing a finger, simply because we love our Danny... Our Dannen...

He is just a young boy, confused and in pain. His eager legs ache to chase the squirrels knocking on the front door, the birds tapping on his window.

Apologies to his playmates, I offer them. Danny cannot come out and play today. He is mending now. Please hold to your hearts... and come back another day.

Now he lies at my side. His brave little body inches closer, his paws upon my feet.

"Do not worry, my son," I said to him after rubbing his head. "Your Daddy is here. No harm will come to you as long as I am near."

He needs me now. Perhaps it's more water or his favorite snack... but I know full well he wants me to lie by him, to hold him and let him know he will be well.

I will bend my knees and kick off these flip flops. I will hold my son.

*

I lie awake in the early sunrise, the quiet of my home having spread her blanket...

My children remain within their dreams.

My young dog Danny blinks at the miracle of a new day, his joy of life my constant teacher.

We spent the evening together for her birthday. We held hands listening to the ocean waves, singing their song to Neptune...

We enjoyed a beautiful dinner in Long Beach... Private moments filled with laughter, a simple touch... a renewal of vows.

The boardwalk beckoned us...

Accepting the invitation we seemed to glide along the wooden runway, the moon our personal escort and the smell of salt air calling us to the shore...

Arriving home we fell into each other's embrace. Looking closely into the eyes of my wife, the mother of my children, I wished her a happy birthday, a wish I have offered her for more than 30 years.

Time has its way with us all... But for her time has been gentle. As I look at her sleep I remember the woman I held in my arms for the first time so long ago... and I find myself once again falling in love.

Kathleen... Thank you for being at my side.

Recognitions

The face of heartbreak is unmistakable. Many of our elderly suffer from great loneliness. They are rejected, abandoned, reduced to objects and cast aside as inconveniences and burdens. They are spoken of but not with, set before televisions for hours and met with indifference. Loved ones complain of them constantly.

My own father died from dementia. He spent his last days lost in his mind, but he was never alone. He was always loved. We bathed him, shaved him and cared for him. It was never a burden... it was a privilege to help my dad. He died knowing he was loved completely.

We are our brothers' keepers. A society that ignores its elderly is a society beginning to die.

Please take the time... Listen from the heart. Speak a gentle word, give a soft kiss... it takes so little but does so much.

*

There are a great people among us, only we do not know it.

They are the poorest of the poor. The unwanted, the uncared for, the rejected, the mentally challenged, the addicts, the blind, the sick and the dying... people who have nothing and no one.

Their very life is a prayer. They intercede for us without knowing it. They suffer, as do we. But can we accept that which *is* without bitterness and resentment?

Suffering is meant to sanctify and burn away the shell of the ego... to set free in the world our divine light.

Can we suffer with great dignity, compassion and love?

*

Firefighters

They are dads and brothers, uncles and sons who have kids, go to ball games and wave our flag proudly. They have bills to pay, weddings and funerals to attend...

But when the siren screams, these amazing men and women run into Hell while others run out. They bravely stand eye to eye with the demon, never flinching.

Their combination of courage, honor and brotherhood is strong and united. They will face any challenge, standing as one...

They battle the cold, the rain, the floods and forest fires...

They entered into the World Trade Center the day evil came to America. They came to rescue their own, the helpless, the trapped and the severely burned.

They came from around the world to answer the call. It is what they were born to do.

It is who they are... Firefighters.

They give their blood, sweat and tears to the unknown faces of the world. They reach across smoke and flame in search of fallen hands, silent cries in burning buildings...

They place their lives at risk for those they have never met, their code of honor one few of us can understand.

They carry their own out of the furnace, their broad shoulders and courageous hearts never wavering. They put it all on the line and stand as one at the gravesides of fallen brothers... brothers who have answered the final call.

They have taken an oath to stand strong, to protect, honor and save life.

Thank you, Firefighters, for being there for my father, brother and me.

When we were at our weakest... you were at our side.

*

Irish People

The Irish people are Warrior Poets...

We enjoy a good cup of tea, a pint or two and a warm hearth, the sound of a fine fiddle, the thunder of a good Irish "reel" and a well written book.

We love our "kin," a sense of humor and good wit.

We will offer a warm handshake, shelter from the storm...

But make no mistake, we are fiercely loyal. We have the courage of a lion and when challenged we will spit in the eye of the devil. We will put a line in the sand and dare you to cross it...

Never mistake our warmth for weakness.

*

Cops: A Funeral

I love to take daily walks. The rain of the day makes no difference. My walking shoes find my feet and my rain slicker my back, my thoughts quiet as the sound of my busy home subsides. Mounds of garbage bags collapse at the curb, gift wrapping and empty cake boxes standing at the top of the piles...

A conversation I had with my son-in-law, a member of the NYPD, floats into my mind.

He had just returned from a funeral, one for Officer Ramos... Detective Ramos, actually, a promotion well deserved but a small comfort for his shattered family, for a wife who will never again hold her husband and for two sons that cry themselves to sleep...

He stood in a sea of blue united with his brothers, white gloves and broken hearts in full salute. He stood among the rank and file. Two of their own had fallen, murdered in cold blood. The sound of the pipers gave his anger and frustration no rest.

We sat and spoke for a while. His heart somber, his eyes glanced west to the streets of Brooklyn. His hand held my daughter's, her courage and pride for her husband a miracle to witness...

I saw the fatigue in his face, his eyes tired and red from grief... I shook his hand. My arms breaking free, a hug from the heart had to be shared. I thanked him for his service. We looked into each other's eyes... Nothing else had to be said.

The night came to a close. Our conversation settled, good night was waved, Christmas gifts found one hand, a black ribbon shield the other...

It is early evening. The rain has just begun. My house lies in the distance. I find myself full of heartbreak and rage. I am thinking of Officer Ramos and Officer Liu. I am thinking of their families, their children. I am thinking of the men and women on post tonight, a constant threat moving nearby. A constant need to stay alert and stay together...

My home comes into view. I say a prayer to my dad, recalling his twenty years on the street, Heaven now his home.... I say a prayer to my Grandpa, his "shield" always on the front lines. I ask them to watch over the guys on patrol, to keep them safe. I ask them to welcome home two of New York City's best... to make room for the heroes.

Let the angels take notice... Two of NYPD's Finest have arrived.

Their colors all blue, their courage and honor unquestioned... their brave souls now at peace.

*

Never confuse the path of peace with avoidance.

It is a journey that demands the courage of personal fearlessness, to take a stand for those who cannot defend themselves... the heartbroken, the elderly, the sick and dying, special needs children, addicts, abused pets and animals... all those forgotten and injured by the world.

*

I meet so many people who show off their guilt like a waving flag.

They move through the world as open wounds, carrying crosses atop their beaten shoulders... They not only bring the darkness of guilt into each moment of their day, they impose the practice of guilt upon their family, friends and even their pets.

They use mental and emotional punishment as whipping posts for past behavior. They lurk behind a perpetual veil of tears... The imposing parent, the constant apologetic wife, the remorseful, sobbing husband...

"I am sorry. Sorry. Please forgive me..." An unending verse.

Lingering around for approval that never arrives, the guilt is repeated, a self-crushing and self-serving act used to crush others...

What is accomplished by self-guilt? What is the need to make others feel guilty? To use it like a blowtorch on exposed skin?

What is its true purpose... what are they *really* trying to do?

*

Psychic Anger

I sat with a mother and grandmother recently. Here were two truly beautiful people enduring the heartbreaking loss of a child.... a handsome young man who could not escape the dark grip of cancer, the tumors in his head offering him no release.

The family gathered at his side, his mom and nana lying with him in bed, their love songs and tear stained kisses whispering into his heart.

They held his hand as they released him to the Angels of Light and Peace. His tired body, only 13 years of age, traveled into eternity... his farewell breaking them into pieces.

As so many do, they sought comfort and healing through the strength of their faith. For some, that is not quite enough.

They needed more to help them through their terrible suffering.

They spent the last four years in search of contact, authentic communication... Their trust was placed in the reputation of "top psychics."

I asked them if they had ever been read before. They said yes... by a very well known "top" psychic. Not someone from television, but one they were encouraged bring their grief to. I asked them how it went.

Terrible, they said.

Nothing made any sense to them.

At first I gave the medium the benefit of the doubt.

Maybe they'd misunderstood. But they said nothing made the slightest bit of sense. I wondered if the medium had been off, possibly having a bad day.

They could maybe accept that, but then they said the psychic told them their child had lived many lives before... and in those past lives this little boy was badly mistreated and hurt by cruel people for generations... that his death from cancer was a release from all of the horrors he had endured.

They were devastated.

Not only were they given no comfort this psychic crushed all of their hope and drove them into despair!

My jaw dropped. My chest was full of rage... How could anyone say that to a grieving mother and grandmother?

It makes me furious to this day.

How dare *anyone* make such statements?

Please be very careful who you expose your grief to. Be thorough in your research. If you are not sure, don't go.

There are some excellent, compassionate mediums out there... be wary of the wannabes, those caught up in fantasy and self-amusement. They can break you in half and destroy your trust and faith in the beauty and peace of true communication.

*

Find the courage to change what must be changed. If you have too much fear, ask for help. There is great strength in true friendship.

Courage arises when you do what must be done despite your fear.

*

I have met people who hold their wallets tighter than their children's hearts.

I have met people who have the time for one more round, one more spin of the wheel, while their children share their worlds with stuffed animals and unmet people on the electric screen.

I have met people who demand the most of their children and offer the least.

People who love to announce the birth of their child and watch them raised by another's hand, children by title, not by touch.

I have met people who measure themselves by their child's accomplishments, basking in the glory and keeping distance in times of failure, using rejection and disappointment like an electric shock.

I have met people who demand respect and worship from their children, the offering of the poor to the tyrant king.

Can you take the time to turn off the noise? Put aside your role?

Sit with your child, any child, and learn of laughter, of living in the moment and of pure joy. Learning to dance in the rain without the umbrella or watching the time, learning to listen to their fears and doubts, tearing down the walls and building bridges to the heart...

Speak little and listen much.

Can you do it?

*

When you meet someone with special needs, someone challenged by the limitations of their bodies, look into their eyes and feel their souls...

Be with them fully.

Do not turn your gaze away. They too are the children of our Beloved Spirit.

You will see within them the miracle of the Creator... and you will pick up your flute and play a love song.

*

Never judge someone's capacity to handle pain, sorrow and grief...

I have met many men who possess great physical strength and other tremendous natural gifts. They have endured hardship in battle, witnessed the losses of brothers in arms, had their limbs removed and been burned horribly...

They have endured the unimaginable and yet, despite their great internal strength, their courage, the loss of a child or a spouse reduces them to darkness... They lay quiet in the dark and their tears are as real as yours. Their suffering is total...

I have met women who have endured the loss of their entire families, their children, their parents... Yet in what seems almost impossible, a feat for giants... they continue to work. They find moments to laugh, to take vacations and keep on going. They do not possess super powers. They have been given the capacity to endure another type of suffering that for most would be unbearable...

They have found peace in the middle of Hell.

We never know what capacity we have to endure pain and sorrow until the moment has arrived. It is only then that you can express yourself as your threshold will allow... Your capacity is not a gift or a weakness. It simply is...

The judgement of others, whether admiration or negative opinion, matters not... It is your path, your suffering that you and you alone can only understand.

Be kind to yourself. Take your time. Find those who understand this law of life. Create distance from those who only offer impatience and the coolness of heart...

Seek those who embrace the flame of your agony, who offer water to the desert of your soul.

Seek those who offer their love without watching the clock, without taking your measure... They are your soul mates who share your joys and help ease your sorrows...

They are the angels you have prayed for.

*

To treat another with dignity requires nothing.

It is a statement of the heart that simply says...

We have all fallen. I honor what is best in you.

Give me your hand. Let me help you stand...

Big Questions

I have met many people who stalk through their days like hunters on the prowl... They seek confrontation as naturally as one requires air. Like an unlit Lucifer match, they wait for just enough friction to ignite their souls. They cast a fishing line into the ocean of humanity, the line of filament tight to the pull and the hook sharp with bite... It pierces deeply into the heart of others.

They seek control, intimidation and fear to gain their place. They leave the broken in their wake.

Have you found yourself hooked into this net?

Or have you seen that the predator of the heart is truly a coward, insecure and that the fear he seeks from you is his only food?

Have you found the strength to stare him in the face?

To know that you are not alone? To know that all good people will offer the swords of their hearts and the shields of their protection to help you...?

Have you found the courage to ask for help... to say "no more?"

*

Why do most people become hostile, defensive or annoyed when their beliefs are challenged?

The Christ figure did just that. He questioned and challenged the rules and beliefs of the day and they crucified him for it.

Have we learned so little, as to not see the great healing that comes from challenging beliefs and questioning blind faith?

He spoke quite clearly.

"You will come to know the truth (abandon beliefs)... and the truth will set you free (enlightenment)!"

*

Whether it is joy or terrible sorrow, it is not *what* you experience in your life; it is *how* you experience it that will bring you to peace and acceptance or anger and fear. Can you be a witness to this?

*

115

Imagine you were given a gift that would allow you to suddenly transform those most evil and cruel...

Your gift would offer them complete release of their evil ways, an evil that completely devours their very being.

Your gift would show them a way out of darkness. They would find complete peace and would never be evil again, even though their evil had personally hurt you or your family.

Would you choose to let evil continue, to let darkness endure?

Or would you choose to eliminate evil and replace it through your gift?

This decision is yours. Not theirs.

*

If you enjoy a color, let's say red...

And your friend, for example, enjoys the color blue...

Have you ever noticed when one of you tries to convince the other that their selection of color is better?

And if one of does not change his or her view, one of you becomes resistant, almost upset that the other does not agree.

Do you find it necessary to be in the right and place the other in the wrong?

Can you fully accept the other's position without the need to diminish their point of view, their choice of thought, while experiencing your point of view without defensiveness or anger?

How often we demand of others to think the way we do or we minimize or complain about their position.

Have you experienced this?

*

Do you find it necessary, perhaps having an internal need, to have to be right which requires that the other person has to be wrong?

Do you unknowingly or even consciously seek out these moments with the kids, the store owner, the PTA or others seeking disagreement for the sake of trying to be right?

Do you take up a cause simply to challenge others?

*

Do you go to bed thinking?

Do you wake up in the morning thinking?

No still moments, no rest for the mind.

Do you have a constant sense of subtle unease, the need or yearn for things to be different?

For you to be elsewhere, other than where you are?

Have you found yourself complaining that the world has treated you unfairly?

*

How often we are drawn in by our "wants?" "Things that we have to have?"

How often, rather than understanding those treasures of life that we truly need?

We want something very badly and we cannot have it? We suffer.

We receive something we truly want... and then become afraid of losing it? We suffer.

We receive something we truly do not want or have not asked for and must accept? We suffer.

We receive something we did not ask for and wish to rid ourselves of it? We suffer.

Hidden underneath the wanting and suffering is a wonderful moment of awakening light.

Can you find it?

Not as a clever thought, mind game, rehearsed explanation or through a carefully disguised revision of another's experience.

Can you truly see why we suffer?

How long does suffering last?

*

What if someone was born on a remote island or a very isolated place and has never been influenced by television, books, bibles or any sacred texts, movies, the internet or any human contact or influence?

Being deprived of all knowledge... would you consider this to be a loss?

*

Do you have thoughts...? Or do thoughts have you?

*

"A starving dog will eat poisoned food."

Have you ever wanted someone to be a part of your life so much that you started to change who you are just to attract them?

Have you ever wanted to be accepted by a group of friends or wanted to be a part of someone's life... when they have shown no interest in you?

Have you ever compromised yourself? Did you do what you knew to be wrong in the deepest part of yourself, just to have someone near you?

Have you ever hungered in your heart for a partner so badly... that you sacrificed yourself in doing so?

I am not speaking of a healthy attraction, of having a teenage crush, wanting to marry or start a family.

I am speaking of a longing, a wanting from deep within the cave of your heart. Emptiness, a lacking, a feeling of desperation, so much so that you cannot experience life without them.

Do you not see that you are doing this to yourself?

Please be careful. Be a guide to your own heart.

Do not let your wanting shatter your dignity. Do not let it destroy your sense of self-respect.

What is this within you?

What is this that drives you?

*

Are you moving towards something?

Or are you moving away from something?

Are you starting something?

Or are you finishing something?

This riddle shows its true face and reveals a thief.

*

Do you prefer beginnings or endings?

For this you cannot choose situations or circumstances to define your answer.

Simply choose and consider.

It has a deep truth within it.

*

Do you have trouble with making apologies, admitting fault, changing your behavior that creates them? Do you have trouble finding the healing process of making amends, the freedom that comes from self-honesty?

Do you find that the art of rationalizing, deflecting, avoidance or finger pointing serves you better? That it maintains your ego defense, which subtly keeps up your false face?

Or can you openly admit your mistakes, work on personal changes, help to correct poor judgements and realize that we as humans err? Are you really willing to dive in and be your own witness to both the good and the bad?

Are you mindful of these personal traits? Have you found self-compassion, a true sense of forgiveness that can only be found in self-love?

Or do you become arrogant and dismissive? Do you point fingers, becoming self-excusing? Do you become defensive, almost blaming others or the situation for your reactions, looking the other way?

Reflect and turn the camera inward.

*

Can you find ten minutes and simply sit still?

Can you be still with yourself, not sleeping, not daydreaming... just still and peaceful?

Can you be at ease with yourself, to be still for ten minutes without watching the clock, without a head full of noise or thought, without music on or running down a list of things to do or forcing yourself to do it?

Can you just be still, silent... present?

Do you find this hard?

Do you find that your thoughts have taken you over?

Do you find that unless you are doing or controlling something you are unable to be at ease?

*

Do you lower your head and drop your eyes because the weight of your world has placed its yoke upon you? And you see your world as dark, heavy, an effort to be lived?

Or do you lower your head and drop your eyes... to witness the joy, the pure happiness in the eyes of a child? The wag of a dog's tail? The gentle purr of a cat's welcome or the awesome scent of a new blossom?

Incomplete

I meet so many people who seem to be looking or searching for something, their eyes always moving about... A great restlessness abides within them, as if they feel incomplete or unfinished...

What is it?

*

There are many who have died who "deserved" life...

And there are many people living who "deserved" to die...

This "thinking" often confuses, frustrates and angers us... yet it happens still and claims much of our soul.

Can you sense that which is past this "thinking?"

Can you go past these "thoughts" and find... peace?

*

Do you enter your day presenting yourself for the acceptance and approval of others, seeking private applause, hoping they take notice...?

Or do you enter your day with a deliberate indifference...?

A "this is me and if they don't' like it... too bad" attitude?

Do you take on a defensive posture, a low level and at times a high intensity flame, ready to take on all comers...?

Or do you enter your day with presence... accepting the moments as they appear? Bringing a true sense of self into each situation without the need to seek approval or disapproval... your actions appropriate and in balance...?

*

Mirror, mirror on the wall...

When you stand alone in front of the mirror, do you feel more comfortable in disguise, in decoration, costume?

Or when you stand alone in front of the mirror, do you feel more comfortable... as exposed, unhidden... revealed...?

Be honest with yourself.

*

So many people I meet are waiting for the weekend, the arrival of summer, to be happy.... for life to show up.

Are you still waiting...?

*

When frustration rises, disappointment calls and rejection has taken over your heart...

Why do you feel the need for self-punishment, increasing the pain or elevating the hurt...?

What does self-harm, self-minimizing... self-anger do for you?

*

When you are alone and quiet... Look into the mirror of your soul without defending yourself.

Do you see that you are at peace with yourself, satisfied with your path, at one... whole?

Or is there a sense of unease, unrest... a sense of being incomplete... a nagging emptiness...?

*

There are many who constantly seek and pursue happiness...

It is a pursuit driven by a sense of unhappiness, that not enough is there, a lack of fulfillment.

Are you constantly seeking happiness...?

Or do you seek the source of your unhappiness... your sense of less...?

*

A Tough Question of Faith

Before the death of a loved one many of us have fallen into prayer, leaning upon on our faith and our religious traditions, to ask for mercy, healing... for a miracle.

Despite our prayers and pleas, many times our loved ones have been called "home," leaving so many of us wounded, unsure and angry because our appeals seemed to have fallen on deaf ears, our pleading leaving us broken...

For others they remain true to their faith and beliefs, accepting the will of their Spirit as it was revealed. They surrender to what has happened, including the wounds of the heart and all the suffering that goes with it...

Has your "faith" increased or decreased when a loved one has died?

*

A Question of Readiness

When we were young and struggling with direction, purpose, heartbreak and love, we often looked to our parents as our closest mentors for advice, counsel and guidance.

We placed our trust in them, believing them to be a light in our darkness. Often their guidance was right. At other times it did not work out so well...

In most cases they did their best and helped as well as they could. We placed a great expectation upon them.

Do you feel ready to accept this responsibility from your own children? From others who trust you?

Or do you feel intimidated and unsure? Is the weight of this task too heavy?

*

A Question of Heights

For some, rising to great heights is exhilarating. Their achievements, successes and their view of life is expanded and filled with awe.

For others...

Great heights create a sense of recklessness and a loss of control. Too much to risk, they see it as a long way to fall.

How do you react to heights?

*

A Question of Return

If you were given a chance to re-live your life over again exactly the way it was... with all the joy and the sorrow, the hopes and all the fears... Would you do it?

Or would you decline?

Would you prefer not to re-live it...? To just let it be and move on until the end of your days...?

*

A Question on the Manner of Death

Many people I meet feel that the manner of death has an impact on the soul and how they enter Eternity... thus the expressions "a good death" or "a bad death."

124

On personal level... what do you feel?

Does it matter how someone dies? Illness? By accident? Self-harm? Harmed by another?

What does the manner of death say to you?

*

A Question of Judgment

Many people hold the idea that moral conduct, both action and thoughts, determines our "afterlife." That our spirit will be rewarded with peace if we have done and behaved well, but if we have acted and thought badly we would be punished.

For some these states are called Heaven and Hell. For others they have been received into illumination, for others the abyss.

Do you believe our behavior is judged? That a final determination will be cast upon us, our life's actions measured? That an "ultimate decision" will put us in our final resting place?

Or do you believe our moral behavior ends with death, that our soul, or consciousness, simply continues? Expanding, learning, shifting into ever changing experiences through eternity?

What do you think? What do you feel?

*

A Question of Courage

For some it takes great courage to remain in a situation that is causing them great anxiety, suffering, pain or dis-ease, that seeing it through is the only choice to make.

For others it takes great courage to leave, to accept that the course they are traveling on will only result in more pain, sorrow and suffering... That despite their efforts no change will come and leaving is the only option.

What is courage to you?

When your fantasies are exposed, demanding that you deal with reality, do you feel happy and free of the make believe?

Or are you upset that your fantasies were revealed?

Do you enter sleep to rest or escape?

If you were to write a heartfelt "message in a bottle" and cast into the "ocean of the universe," who would you like to receive it?

What message would you like delivered...?

It has often been stated that God has a plan for us.

This of course includes beautiful, wonderful events and discoveries in our lives...

And yet...

It also includes great heartbreak, horrific sorrow and despair.

Do you believe there is a "plan" in place?

Or is it the unfolding of life as it happens?

If you do not seek peace, then what do you seek?

Why do you continue to hurt yourself?

There are those who enjoy the quiet of the early dawn sunrise, the still hum before the noise of the world comes into play... Their souls awaken with daybreak.

For others... they enjoy nightfall, the light cast by starlight and the resting sun. Moon beams light their path and darkness, an old and comfortable friend, calls to them.

Are you a child of the dawn? Or a child of the night?

*

A false sense of peace comes from the illusion of control...

This sense of power imposed on one's self and others creates living slaves of the heart.

Is that what you seek...?

What are you trying to control?

*

In a very famous Japanese wood block print there is an image of a large boulder.

Solid, firm, imposing... It is a Zen symbol of the depth of meditation. Around it are the flowing waters of a river, ever traveling. Impermanence, forming and reshaping... it is a constant movement.

Does your inner soul feel more connected to the boulder or the water?

*

The ever movement of thought amid the mind streams...

Do you find yourself drifting into the past, revisiting memories and thinking of what was or what should have been?

Or do you find yourself imagining the future... projecting what might be or what might become? Where does your mind move most?

127

*

Can you identify, for yourself or someone you care about...?

When you feel upset, a sense of dis-ease, panic or fear, do you find that you withdraw? Do you go quiet and distance yourself, pushing all others away? Do you blame, point fingers, yell...? Do you declare you will handle it alone, regardless of how your behavior has become or how you are acting to those around you?

Or do you seek to share your burdens? Do you openly tell all who will listen what has happened to you, what you have to deal with? Your pain, your sorrow, your troubles... all your issues? You pull all into your circle of upheaval, seeking to be rescued, taking on the role of constant victim... letting loose a never ending stream of complaint?

*

There are those who sincerely apologize, who make every effort to change their behavior and paths of action...

And yet members within the family, the spouse, children, parents and others offer no forgiveness, no opportunity for renewal...

What to do then? What to do?

*

Have you found out why you feel the need to try to control everything and everyone you come into contact with?

*

No matter where you go...

No matter what you do...

You will be there.

Can you keep good company with yourself?

Or are you always looking to escape from the moment, hoping to meet a different you, looking for the future to rescue you?

*

The video game Pac Man took its name from the Japanese word "senppaku," which means "you are what you eat or take in."

What are you feeding your head?

Do you feel well and at peace or uneasy and unsettled?

Does what you "eat" draw you into oneness... or push you out?

Answer from the gut!

*

We all have loved ones who have died and crossed over... There is so much emotion.

Distraction, grief, fear, relief, anger...

So often I meet wonderful people who carry in their hearts private thorns, aches, a constant vibration of frustration...

"I wish I had said" this or "I wish I had done" that, they say to me. They carry this with them for years, sometimes decades, an unseen weight pressing on their souls.

How have you coped with these feelings?

This pain and unease endures in many.

*

When you have had enough... then what?

*

Which is more painful... the physical exercise of muscles? Or the mental exercise of feeling?

*

For some, it is a constant passion to maintain *what is*, requiring diligent effort, control, and organization.

For others, they seem to accept what unfolds as it comes. They don't resist the shifts and changes.

They seem to be saying "it as it is."

Are you trying to keep "it" together...?

Or are you letting "it fall away as it comes?"

*

How truly willing are you to face your fears?

About the Author

ROBERT E. HANSEN was born in Bay Ridge, Brooklyn, New York into an Irish Catholic and law enforcement family. Shortly after, he and his family moved to Long Island where he attended Cure of 'Ars Catholic School. Later, he attended Mepham High School, excelling in football, wrestling and track. He earned a degree in Education (Elementary and Psychology) from CW Post College.

Robert has studied martial arts since he was 11. At age 21 the Department of Treasury hired him to be their defensive tactics teacher. In this capacity he would soon find himself working with the Nassau County Police Department, NYPD, the FBI and the Secret Service. In 1972 he opened his first martial arts school in Baldwin NY. Some years later, his prowess was honored by Black Belt Magazine with three consecutive "National Instructor of the Year" awards.

Robert studied Zen Buddhism at the New York Zendo Shobo-Ji in Manhattan and Dai Bosatsu Zendo Kongo-Ji monastery in the Catskill Mountains.

In addition, he spearheaded the largest program on Long Island for children with special needs. This program ran from 1987 until he retired from it in 2005. The program helped thousands of children with multiple physical disabilities, as well as autism and cerebral palsy.

Around 1993 Robert's gift of mediumship materialized quite unexpectedly. He meditates daily, which has been a catalyst in nurturing his psychic abilities.

Robert is married with four children and recently became a grandfather. He is a huge sports fan (especially hockey and football).